Our Best War Stories

Prize-winning Poetry & Prose
from the
Col. Darron L. Wright
Memorial Awards

Christopher Lyke, editor
Middle West Press LLC
Johnston, Iowa

Literary Collections / General / American
Fiction / War & Military
"Our Best War Stories" – Christopher Lyke, editor
ISBN (print): 978-1-953665-55-3
ISBN (e-book):978-1-953665-00-3
Library of Congress Control Number: 2020917267

Middle West Press LLC
P.O. Box 31099
Johnston, Iowa 50131-9428
www.middlewestpress.com

Special thanks to military-writing patrons
James Burns of Aurora, Colo.
and Aramis Calderon of Safety Harbor, Fla.
Learn more at: www.aimingcircle.com

Cover Design
Paul Hewitt / Battlefield Design
URL: www.battlefield-design.co.uk

Other Military-themed Books from
Middle West Press LLC

poetry

Welcome to FOB Haiku:
War Poetry from Inside the Wire,
by Randy Brown, a.k.a. "Charlie Sherpa"

Hugging This Rock:
Poems of Earth & Sky, Love & War
by Eric Chandler

Permanent Change of Station
by Lisa Stice

Proving Ground
by Lynn Marie Houston

non-fiction

Reporting for Duty:
U.S. Citizen-Soldier Journalism
from the Afghan Surge, 2010-2011
Edited by Randy Brown

Why We Write:
Craft Essays on Writing War
Edited by Randy Brown
& Steve Leonard

Table of Contents

2020

Introduction

By Christopher Lyke, editor, *Line of Advance*

In 2013, Matt Marcus and I started *Line of Advance*, an on-line journal we hoped would one day become *The Paris Review* of veterans' literature. At the time, it seemed a pretty lofty objective for two guys sitting in a dive bar on Chicago Avenue.

Thankfully, organically, the idea evolved into something else. Instead of an ivory tower, it became more like a patrol base, a camp from which we and our fellow writers could launch.

The metaphor is apt: Marcus and I first met as Illinois Army National Guard citizen-soldiers, deployed to Combat Outpost Najil, a small base overlooking three valleys in Eastern Afghanistan's Laghman Province. There were 50 or so of us there, sharing few creature comforts, and just as many Afghan National Army.

When there was downtime–precious little there was–Matt and I took notes, sketches really, of what we were experiencing. Because I was a squad leader, I received all the mission briefs, locations, and other paperwork documenting our experiences. All of that went into the footlocker for the trip home. Matt and I knew, without talking about it at the time, that eventually we'd be writing about Afghanistan.

What we didn't know was how our words would find readers.

That, of course, was before our barstool lightning bolt. First as a subscription-based e-book, and later as a free website, *Line of Advance* became a location from which we and our fellow writer-veterans would operate. Ralph Waldo Emerson talked of speaking in "words as hard as cannon balls," and I tend to side with him. We offer contributors room to grow, to experiment, and to improve–but we also edit for excellence. We want not only to help veterans write, but to write *well*.

The terrain for veterans' writing has become richer in the past decade, and more complex. There are increasingly more venues–including general-interest publications–open to military and military-adjacent authors. We like to think that *Line of Advance* has been part of the vanguard in achieving such acceptance, and that we help continue to lead the way in connecting writer-veterans and readers.

The fight for recognizing veterans' stories and achievements in literature isn't over, of course. Over the years, we seem to have collected a squad–maybe even a platoon–of fellow travelers. Writers such as Eric Chandler, Brian Kerg, Randy Brown, and other *Line of Advance* alumni keep each other updated and amused through social media, e-mail, and telephone. Others, such as Sarah Maples, Ryan Stovall, and William Upton, are less-often heard from, but kind enough to regularly send us new work.

For our editors, each poem or story can simultaneously feel like a letter from home, and a message from a distant outpost. We are proud to call these artists sisters and brothers. We want to extend that literary fellowship to even more writers, and to share their words to ever-increasing audiences.

In this, nothing has been more important than the support of the Blake & Bailey Family Fund. Since 2016, the Georgia-based philanthropic organization has underwritten the Col. Darron L. Wright Memorial Writing Awards, an annual contest recognizing the poetry and prose of current and past U.S. service members.

Administered by *Line of Advance*, the awards commemorate a U.S. Army leader and author who was killed in a September 2013 parachute training accident. Darron L. Wright, 45, had deployed three times to Iraq, and was author of a 2012 memoir titled *Iraq Full Circle: From Shock and Awe to the Last Combat Patrol in Baghdad and Beyond.* Army veteran and poet F.S. Blake, author of two chapbooks of his own, is a past contributor to *Line of Advance*. On page 5 of this anthology, Blake offers his personal remembrances of Wright.

In the short time since its inception, the Col. Darron L. Wright Memorial Awards have become a leading indicator of excellence in "veterans' literature." Past winners and finalists have gone on to further recognitions and accomplishments. To name just a few:

Outdoor sports writer, U.S. Air Force Academy graduate, and F-16 fighter pilot Eric Chandler published his first collection of poetry, *Hugging This Rock*, in 2017.

Earlier this year, U.S. Marine Corps veteran Dewaine Farria, author of the novel *Revolutions of All Colors*, was named winner of the inaugural Syracuse University Press Veterans' Writing Award for best book-length fiction or non-fiction.

Former U.S. Army Ranger Ray McPadden was winner of the American Library Association's W.Y. Boyd Award for Excellence in Military Fiction, for his 2018 novel *And the Whole Mountain Burned*.

Also earlier this year, U.S. Naval Academy graduate and former surface warfare officer Travis Klempan published his first novel *Have Snakes, Need Birds*.

With the Blake & Bailey Family Fund's continued assistance, we expanded the Wright Awards in 2020. Now included are categories for prose and poetry written by family members of U.S. service members and veterans. Katey Schultz, author of the 2013 short-story collection *Flashes of War*, and the 2019 Afghan War novel *Still Come Home*, graciously served as our guest judge for all catetories. And we partnered with veteran-owned independent publisher Middle West Press LLC to produce this anthology.

We're proud to note an increasing diveristy of life-experiences and voices in our 2020 Wright Awards. For example, U.S. Army veteran John Thampi, winner of our veterans' poetry category, was invited to attend the 2019 Oxford Brookes Veterans Workshop. His work has been featured on BBC Radio and elsewhere. Former U.S. Navy officer Jillian Danback-McGhan, who took first-place in our veteran prose category, is publishing her first stories in print this year–but is already navigating toward a collection of short-fiction.

Family-category prose-winner Desiree Cooper is, among other accomplishments, a Pulitzer Prize-nominated journalist. And, with a number of poetry collections and chapbooks to her credit, family-category poetry winner Lisa Stice is a widely published observer of life as a military spouse and parent.

The *Line of Advance* has evolved considerably from those first days in Afghanistan and on Chicago Avenue. Like the writers it features– and like the city in which it's published–it always strives to do better, but never apologizes for itself. That's how a thing like this should be. War stories are stories about people, after all; about the small moments when we each realize that we are alive, and part of something beautiful, and terrible, and painfully human.

Thank you for reading this anthology. Thank you for more than seven years of *Line of Advance*. Thank you for five years of the Col. Darron L. Wright Memorial Writing Awards. We look forward to reading and sharing your words, for many more years to come.

See you "on the line"!

Christopher Lyke is a writer and teacher living in Chicago. He served in Afghanistan and Africa as an enlisted infantry soldier with the U.S. Army. He edits and publishes Line of Advance, *an on-line literary journal for veterans. He can usually be found running with his dog in Logan Square or watching the Buckeyes at Vaughan's Pub. Lyke's work has been featured in such venues as* BlazeVOX *and* Military Experience & the Arts' *literary journal* As You Were. *In 2015, he won the short-story award in* Proud to Be: Writing by American Warriors, Vol. 4.

Darron L. Wright:
"Write Big to Be Big"
By F.S. Blake

"Baller's dead." Alex barked quickly into the phone, as if we were still back in Iraq, working on a battalion staff, coordinating a mechanized infantry fight in the middle of the Sunni Triangle. Quick details followed. Fifteen seconds later, he hung up. It was all he had to say.

Col. Darron L. Wright, 45, was a self-made warrior and scholar. He deployed to Iraq three times, then wrote a book about it: *Iraq Full Circle: From Shock and Awe to the Last Combat Patrol in Baghdad and Beyond*. A favorite snapshot features Wright in the darkness of early morning twilight, on the Iraq-Kuwait border. It is 2010. He is wearing a sage-green combat shirt, while readying to mount up again with 4th Stryker Brigade, 2nd Infantry Division for the final convoy out of Iraq. He is not wearing a helmet. His hair is close-cropped and his expressive, bushy eyebrows are each open question marks. He has lit a cigar in celebration. It is the last combat patrol in Iraq.

Wright was killed in a September 2013 parachute training accident at Fort Bragg, N.C. He had been newly assigned as assistant chief of staff in the XVIII Airborne Corps, and was preparing to deploy to Afghanistan. He was survived by a wife and three children, as well as a large cohort of soldiers and citizens—peers and colleagues at all levels, who count themselves better people because of his influences.

All great stories are built on strong characters, and I've never met or read of a character that could rival that of Wright. I served with him when he was a major, when he was assigned as the operations officer for the 1st Battalion, 8th Infantry Regiment out of Fort Carson, Colorado. In the Army, the operations officer (referred to as the "S3") is the lead dog on staff. Other battalion staff functions include personnel (S1), intelligence (S2), logistics (S4), and communications (S6). For each significant event—every mission—the S3 is responsible for the results from a deliberate, standardized Army planning process. After inputs from other "S" sections, the S3's assistants curate and publish the written "operations order." These standardized, 5-paragraph documents translate a commander's intent into executable instructions and actions, step by step, unit by unit, function by function. The S3 officer's task is to make order out of chaos, in word and in deed.

In spring 2003, our unit had been deployed to Al Diwaniyah, Iraq, 180 kilometers south of Baghdad, and was conducting combat operations on a small Tigris River peninsula deep in the Sunni Triangle. The analogy Wright later used to describe his arrival as the new S3 was that it was like performing a spinal transplant on an Olympic sprinter without losing a split-second of speed. Wright met the transition with enthusiasm and a wide Texas grin. As our unit struggled in the oppressive heat of Iraq, the staff got our first taste of our new lead character.

Six-foot-tall and broad-shouldered, Darron was an imposing presence. Because our battalion commander, Lt. Col. Nate Sassaman, had played quarterback for West Point in the 1980s, it was rumored that our new S3 had been his running back. Not only was Wright built like one, but the mutual rapport, complementary skill sets, and locker-room banter he shared with the commander seemed to support the rumor's veracity.

"[Wright] was responsible not only for the day-to-day fight, but for the long-range planning as well," writes Sassaman in his 2008 memoir *Warrior King, a Commander's Triumph and Betrayal in Iraq*. "It was the fighting, though, that Darron relished. This was a kid who could almost smell out the contact."

Wright was a beast! A proud member of the "350-pound Bench-press Club," he was intimidating and dominant. Citing the power of inputs and outputs, Wright taught us to "eat big to be big." He challenged us to get "war big"–to use what little personal time we had to constantly improve ourselves, physically and mentally. And he encouraged us to enjoy the fruits of home, to keep our spirits up. He boiled his own worldly needs, for example, down to an essential "3 Rs": "Red Bull, Red Vines, and Red Man." More than once, his tactical bulletpoof vest suffered from a stray splat of tobacco spit.

Contrary to the rumors, Wright had not first met Sassaman on the grid-iron. Rather than a 4-year West Point "ring knocker," Wright had developed his intellect and abilities in a series of stair-steps. Wright was born in Dallas, but grew up in nearby Mesquite. In high school, he joined the Army National Guard. As Sassaman notes in his book, Wright was "a tough-talking Texan through-and-through. [...] If it wasn't from Texas, or didn't involve Texas in some way, it wasn't worth much. To Darron, the world revolved around [University of Texas] football, UT basketball, and the Dallas Cowboys."

After high school, Wright attended Kemper Military College in Booneville, Missouri, and earned an associate degree and commission as a U.S. Army second lieutenant in 1988. In 1991, Wright earned a bachelor's degree in criminal justice from the University of North Texas, Denton. In 2002, just before he transferred to Fort Carson, Colorado, he earned a master's degree in Strategic Studies and National Security Decision-Making from the United States Naval War College, Newport, Rhode Island.

Despite his physicality, Wright was generally jovial and approachable, full of friendly greetings, most of which were punctuated by "Airborne." (Examples: "Good morning! Airborne!" and "Hey there, Airborne!") His North Texas twang was a non-lethal weapon, disarming and charming opponents, while also partially camouflaging his status as a cerebral juggernaut.

Wright had mastered his military craft through memorization of doctrine and process, but it was the way he applied data that set him apart. His mindset was world-class. He could quickly analyze information about people and problems, and apply his conclusions rapidly and decisively. Best of all, he did so in ways that made everyone in his orbit want to follow his lead. Wright was a leader on the battlefield, and in every room into which he ever stepped foot.

When a few of us gathered after the funeral, we brainstormed ways we could keep Wright's influence and memory alive. Among the many colorful and quotable "Darronisms" was: "a simple plan doesn't make you a simple leader." Wright's straightforward, no-nonsense, lead-by-doing approach was the hallmark of his tactical and problem-solving genius—and now serves as a guiding principle for the literary prize that bears his name. It is a simple idea, commemorating a complex man.

In his own book's prologue, Wright noted, "Every soldier has a personal story, family, and issues that make up the human aspect of war." Thanks to his example, many of Wright's fellow "Fighting Eagles" are now authors in their own rights. "Big Baller," as we grew to call him, showed us the ways that writing can help organize complex thoughts and emotions and experiences of war. It can generate growth and healing. It can outfight and outlast even death.

I'd like to say a special thank-you to Wright's family for allowing us the privilege of attaching the name of Darron L. Wright to this award, and for trusting us to carry his legacy and memory forward. We hope he would be proud of the results.

Thank you also to the *Line of Advance*, and in particular its founding editor Chistopher Lyke, for growing the Darron L. Wright Memorial Writing Awards into the prestigious recognition that it is today.

And, finally, thank you to our writers and readers, for their respective contributions. Through this fellowship, we appreciate the opportunity to gather and to reflect upon our memories of a good man, and stories of his character.

"Hook 'em."

–F.S. Blake,
Summer 2020

F.S. Blake is a member of the Blake & Bailey Family Fund. A writer and U.S. Army veteran, his poetry has been published in such literary journals as As You Were, O-Dark-Thirty, *and* Wrath-Bearing Tree. *He has published two chapbooks of poetry including work related to war and military service:* Terminal Leave *(2018) and* Above the Gold Fields *(2019), each from Finishing Line Press. He was nominated for a Pushcart Prize in 2018. For more information about his writing, visit: www.fsblake.com.*

2016

The Stay

By David R. Dixon
First-Place Prose, 2016

Where I grew up, I knew a lot of farmers. The oldest and most experienced of them seemed to have an amazing ability when it came to the weather. Their understanding of nature was so great it seemed as if they could almost speak weather into or out of existence, as if they could bargain with the Earth itself.

When I asked them about it, how they could know the weather so well–it seemed as if they were not merely predicting nature, but commanding it. They gave me all kinds of explanations: "I can feel it in my bones" or "see them cows layin' down over there?" or "my daddy used to tell us …" or "can't you smell it?" or "once you been out here long enough, you just know."

I never understood how those old timers could do that. I still don't.

My uncanny knack for prediction, my own esoteric knowledge of the cosmos–my gift, if you can call it that–is of a slightly different nature than the weather.

I sense Death.

I can hear it, smell it, see it–taste it, even–in a way others cannot. I don't know why, but I do know when. I remember the first time it happened, half a world away and years ago. I remember when I first discovered I knew, just like the farmer, things that others did not. And that–just like like the old farmer with the rain–I could bargain with the universe, argue with it, and even forestall it.

But the universe is implacable. No matter the relationship the farmer has with the thunderstorm, he cannot delay it forever. And, no matter my relationship with Death–that most patient and personal of natural forces–it can only be delayed for a time.

People often avoid thinking about that truth until the end of their lives, until it's too late to matter, until they realize they don't fear death but more the possibility of eternal regret–regret of things done and not done, of words said and not said, of chances wasted and paths untaken, of lives out of balance like an overdrawn bank account.

Death arrives with a ledger not its own, and whether or not we are ready, it is there to collect. It is not Death we owe: Death measures us against ourselves. Death is only the messenger. The final value is measured at that instant: Did we do enough with what we had to leave a net positive? Do our victories outweigh our regrets? Is the measure of our lives a sum or a difference?

I've seen all kinds of people go.

I've seen people whose lives are so far in the red they'd have to live a thousand years to make it right.

I remember one of those–it's been two years now–a man in a car accident on Grove Road, at the intersection just before the interstate. He must have fallen asleep or something, because his pickup had drifted across the lanes and he'd hit a transfer carrying a load of railroad ties head on. His F-150 never stood a chance.

I'd been driving around all night, like I usually do, listening for Death's quiet-but-not-quite-silent footsteps. I can, like that old farmer with the rain, hear Death, when I listen for it. At first I had to strain to hear its approach, had to sit silent and still to the point of emotional exhaustion, to hear Death's ghostly tread. By this point, however, like the farmer, I'd been out there long enough to just know.

I was first on the scene, well before the paramedics and the police. I could sense Death lingering there–waiting for me, I like to think. The transfer truck driver was out of his cab, staring at the man trapped underneath the big rig in the wreckage of the Ford. The trucker's eyes were bulging wide and white in the darkness.

"He–I swear to God–I don't–I mean, he was ... was ... was in his lane and then–all of a sudden, man–I–Jesus Christ–he just came over so fast," the trucker stuttered.

I nodded. "It happens, man; it happens. You call the police yet?" I try to get everyone else away when I work. Giving people something useful to do helps them get over the trauma more quickly.

"Ah–uh, no–I mean ... *Shit*–I better call," the man muttered. "I was just trying ... trying to see if there was an-anything I could ... uh, *do*–you know?" he finished, voice rising, looking for approval, for comfort, for assurance that everything was going to be all right.

I nodded again. "Yeah, I know. I'll take care of him, OK?" I told him gently. "You call 911 and set out some flares so no one else wrecks out here."

The trucker nodded and climbed back up into the rig. I saw his face lit by his cell phone screen as I knelt by the driver's side of the destroyed pickup. I could feel Death's presence, impatient and almost annoyed. No doubt there were other appointments to keep that night.

I'm sure the schedule is always full.

Where the transfer truck ended and the pickup truck began was hard to say. The two vehicles were intertwined like teenage lovers, all interlocked curves and sharp angles. The pavement was wet with leaking fluids, and shards of broken glass sparkled like blood diamonds in the moonlight.

I reached into the mass of wreckage and felt a blood-slicked hand grasp mine.

"Can you hear me?" I asked only as loudly as it would take for whoever was inside to hear.

"Y-yes," rasped a man's voice, bewildered and afraid. "Wh-what hap-happened?" I shook my head at the question. So often, it's the same: everyone looking for reason, for justification, as if they somehow expected the universe to admit it had erred—as if they could demand redress from fate.

"I don't know," I told him. "It doesn't really matter now, does it?"

"N-no ... I guess not."

"Listen to me," I said, "I am going to help you, but–"

"You a doctor?" he croaked. "You going to get me out of here?"

"No," I told him softly but with careful solemnity. "No I am not. You are not going to get out, but–"

The man whimpered. "But ... G-get ..." The man coughed a wet cough and I felt Death lean closer. "Get me out! I don't want t-to–"

"To die?" I asked. "Very few do, when it comes down to it—even people who've lived a good life. There's nothing anybody can do about it, though. Not even a doctor."

I paused and squeezed his hand. This next part is always the most difficult for people to understand. "As long as you are holding onto my hand," I told him, "you won't die, OK? You can't die as long as I'm touching you, but–"

"Don't let go!" he cried. "Don't let me go!"

"I have to," I told him. "I can't hold Death off permanently—it'll be my time to die someday, too, you know? Can't hold your hand forever."

The man sobbed.

"Listen to me," I said. "I told you I would help, and I will, OK? Tell me what you want me to do after this. Tell me and I'll do it. Do you–"

"Ho-hold my hand–" the man snapped. "Don't let me die!"

"I told you," I reminded him, "I can't do that but for so long. Think about what I said. What do you want me to do? Most people don't get this chance. Don't waste it! Think about it. You tell me what you want, and I'll do it."

There was silence. There usually is.

Finally, the man sniffed from inside the wreck. "I ... I ... Do you know ... Phillip Mackey?"

"No," I told him. "But I can find him."

"OK," the man said. "OK. Find him and ... and tell him I'm sorry. Tell him I never-never-shoulda run his daughter off from the church. Tell him I was wrong when ... ." The man trailed off but resumed with renewed vigor. "I was wrong when I done it, and I knew it–even ... even then. You tell him I done a lot of things I regretted, but nothing more than that. You hear me?"

"I hear you," I replied. "Is Phillip gonna know what church you're talking about?"

The man sobbed again. "Ye-yeah ... He'll know. I ... I'm Jim Hicks. I ... I was his preacher when his youngest–Stephanie–got pregnant and she wasn't married. I ... I preached hellfire and damnation for three ... three Sundays. Stephane? Shh–she ran away and ... next thing–" the man sobbed and couldn't finish.

I felt Death overpowering me, reaching into the truck, desperate to pry Hicks' hand loose from my grip. I squeezed more tightly–it wasn't time, not yet.

"Do you want me to tell Stephanie you're sorry, too?" I asked him.

"You can't!" the man in the truck wailed. "You can't! Not no more, not unless ..." he sobbed. "I guess maybe I can tell her myself ... if the Lord'll let me ..."

"OK," I said softly. "I understand. I'll find Mackey and tell him."

I took a deep breath. Now came the most difficult part.

"I'm going to let go, now, all right?" I told him.

"What happens then?" the man asked, less panic in his voice than curiosity. "What happens after ... after you let go? I die ... y-you said that–but then what?" I shrugged. I have never thought of an answer better than the truth, despite all the times I've been asked.

"I don't know," I told him.

"O-Okay," the man said.

I gave his hand a final squeeze and he returned it. He let go first–which made it easier. I let go and our hands separated.

I heard the man sigh and felt the eerie presence of Death–that eternal champion–as it swept past me. Then the presence was gone, and I knew Jim Hicks was gone with it.

I always tell people they've got a chance most don't, and it's true.

What I don't tell them is the other truth–that it doesn't usually do any good. If a life is as far in arrears as some folks', a stranger coming out of the blue to apologize to a wronged wife or say "I love you" to an underappreciated former boyfriend rarely means much. Like Shakespeare said, "the evil that men do lives after them; the good is oft interred with their bones."

As soon as I said the name Jim Hicks to Phillip Mackey, he slammed the door in my face.

I can only tip the scales but so much.

Not everybody is taken with his life's ledger in the red, though. I've been fortunate enough to stave off death for a moment for some mighty deserving folks, too.

I remember a young kid in the hospital just last week. I usually don't go to hospitals because it's just too much–I can't make it everywhere, and when I'm talking to one person I can feel Death all around me, taking people here and there. I wind up rushing, and that's not right. That's worse than not being there at all.

It kills me, I'd say, if it weren't so ironic.

Last week, though, I felt Death beckon me, felt it reach out and nudge me with a bony finger and bid me follow. I did, and wound up at Saint Francis, stalking the halls while Death made regular visits behind the doctors and checked the same charts and graphs.

I found myself led to a room on the third floor. I knew I was only a few steps ahead, so I pushed the door open and let myself in. The room was full of cellophane balloons wishing the boy well. There was flower arrangement after flower arrangement. Stacks of cards from family and classmates. The scene had the standard hospital soundtrack: the soft hum of electronics and the rhythmic, muted *beep beep* of various monitors. A young black boy of 13 or 14 lay in the bed, skin gray and body thin and flushed with sweat.

I remembered hearing on the local news about three boys who'd gotten meningitis. I could sense the coming dark and knew the boy and I weren't alone.

When he heard the door open, his eyes fluttered open. Death took a step back and I had a mental image of it waiting just outside the door.

"Hey," the boy said, voice flat and drained.

"Hey," I said. "Listen ... Do you mind if I hold your hand?"

He nodded. "Yeah, you can–I'm not contagious. That's what they say, but you know how that goes ... It's good to have somebody here, you know? My mom is usually, but ... she's with my sister right now ... Jayla's afraid to come up here ..." I smiled and started to speak but he continued. "She's not afraid, 'cause, uh, she thinks she's gonna get sick. It's just, she ... She don't want to see me like this, you know?"

I took his hand. His grip was weak.

"I understand, I really do. What's your name?" I don't always ask, but this time I did.

"Marcus–but most everybody calls me Marc, 'cept for my mom."

"OK, Marc, I'm Will," I told him. "Listen, I don't know how to tell you this–" I began.

"You a preacher?" Marc interrupted. "I know I'm gonna die, OK? It isn't gonna scare me, all right? I'm way past that, you know? I'm young, but that don't make me dumb."

I smiled as bravely as I could. It was rare to find somebody like this– sometimes, I swear they help me more than I help them. "OK, Marc, you got me. I'm not a preacher, though, but that is kind of what I was gonna say."

"C'mon man, I know what's up," he said with a twinkle in his eye, as if he'd gotten the best of me.

"But, it's not that simple," I told him. "Thing is, Marc, I have kind of this ... *gift*, you could say. I know when people are going to die." I remember getting a lump in my throat, which is kind of crazy considering I can't even begin to count the number of times I'd had this exact conversation. "Marc, you're going to go when I let go of your hand–but not until then, all right? I can't hold your hand forever so–"

"'Course you can't," Marc agreed. "You got to live too, you know? You can't just park it up here for the rest of your life. But ... if I go when you do, can you at least hold on 'til my mom gets back up here? And maybe she can bring Jayla in too?"

"Yeah," I told him, "I can hold on for that long. I tell you what else—you tell me what you want me to do for you after … after I let go. And I'll do it. Anything."

"I told Jayla I was gonna fix the basketball hoop in front of the garage," he said without hesitation. "Me and K from down the street broke it by accident a coupla months ago and I never … never did get it put back up for her. You promise you gonna fix it?"

"I swear I'll fix it, Marc. I swear," I told him.

We sat around for a few more minutes and talked about the NBA Finals. When I told him the Clippers had beaten the Spurs in Game 7 the night before, he laughed. "I told K that Tim Duncan was too old!" Marc said with as much glee as his ragged body could muster. "I told him, but he's always all over Tim Duncan!"

The door opened to admit a weary, well-dressed black woman who could only have been Marc's mother. She arched her eyebrow at me and opened her mouth—no doubt to justifiably ask who the hell I was—when her son spoke first.

"Hey, Mom, this is Will. We been talking about the Finals. Did you know the Spurs lost? Make sure you tell K I told him they wasn't gonna make it this year—don't let him tell you he said it too, 'cause he didn't."

"OK, baby, I will," she told him plaintively. "You OK?"

He smiled. "No, Mom, I really ain't … Hey, listen—for real—I don't think I'm gonna be around much longer … I want to see Jayla, OK? Tell her it's important."

"Baby, baby, Marcus, you're gonna be OK, all right?" The woman was in tears. "You're gonna make it, don't say that!"

"Mom," Marc said with a sigh, "just please go get Jayla, OK?"

Marc's mother dabbed her eyes with a tissue and disappeared outside the door. "You can let go now," Marc told me.

"But—But—You said you wanted to see Jayla!" I protested.

"I didn't say I was gonna let go, Will," he told me with a weak grin. "But when I go, I'm gonna go out when I wanna go, not when you say. It's gonna be my call, not yours."

"All right, whatever you say, Marc," I told him and let go. I felt Death slip in the door without knocking, and knew it stood next to us, waiting. Marc held my hand.

The door opened again and Marc's mom came back with a tall, slender girl who looked to be 7 or 8, braids and beads in her hair. The girl's face was streaked with tears. "Jayla," Marc said. "You gonna make it, OK, girl? I'm gonna be watching out for you, you know? You got to listen to Mom, all right, 'cause I'm not gonna ... ah, *be* there, you know? So do what she says and study hard ... you *hearin'* me?"

Jayla nodded.

"Good. This is Will," Marc said with a nod to me. "He's gonna fix the basketball goal up for you–he told me he would–and make sure you practice every day–I'm gonna' be watchin' from up *there*." He pointed with his other hand to the ceiling. "And I wanna see you wearin' that garnet and black when you get to college, all right? I wanna see you out there on the court, got it?"

"Marcus, baby ..." his mom said, sobbing.

"It's gonna be all right, Mom," Marc said. As his mom and Jayla leaned in to hug him, he let go of my hand to put his arm around them. Startled, I reached to grab his hand, but Marc moved too quickly.

Just before the heartrate monitor went off, Marc nodded to me.

The nurses rushed in and I grabbed his hand but to no avail. A doctor shooed me out of the room and I found myself in the hallway. I got Marc's address off a card attached to some flowers on a cart outside the room.

The hoop was up that afternoon.

I don't know if Jayla will play basketball in college or even go to college. I just don't know. All I know is that I tried to help.

People often say that knowledge is power, but that's not exactly true. I learned that first-hand a decade ago, in a sweltering palm grove next to an irrigation canal, southeast of an insignificant Iraqi town named Tarmiyah.

I never saw the artillery rounds, tucked in like sleeping vipers underneath a fallen palm tree.

I felt something though, a second before it all happened. It was the first time in my life I realized Death's presence, and in all the years since, it was still the most intense I've ever felt it. I could almost see the scythe, could almost smell the dank must of the crypt. I felt Death's tattered shroud as it swept over me. Marquez was right beside me cursing Iraq's spring heat when the world exploded.

I wound up a half-dozen feet away, ears ringing, blood stinging my eyes, right arm twisted at a grotesque angle, my helmet gone God knows where, my rifle snatched from my hands and tossed into the palm groves by the power of the blast. My right leg was still attached but my uniform was solid red below the thigh. I struggled for breath. I felt like Atlas himself was standing on my chest. I moved my arm to try to push myself up but realized that as badly broken as it was, it couldn't sustain any weight.

A voice called out and I managed to pick my head up.

Marquez lay beside me, moaning, in the shallow IED crater.

The blast had ripped him to shreds. His legs were gone and his right arm was a mass of tendons and bone and sinew at the shoulder. His face was burnt and his eyes swelled shut; his short black hair was matted with blood. Marquez mouthed something and his left hand reached out to me, grasping for something–anything. As I took his left hand as best I could with my damaged right, a shadow passed over us.

Above us stood Death, impossibly tall and dark in the sun-drenched palm grove. Somehow I understood, that while Death was looking at me, it was there for Marquez. I held Marquez's hand. I knew–I just *did*–that as long as I held his hand, Marquez would stay with us. Death was waiting, yes. But it would wait.

I heard a voice. It was Harper, the platoon medic. "Shit! Shit! Shit!" he shouted. "Smith! Sergeant Sims! Help me out over here! Daniels and Marquez are hit bad over here, man!"

I heard Lieutenant Roberts yell back: "Doc, I need Smith over here with me workin' on Lee! Can you spare him?"

I don't remember the answer, but I do remember Harper and somebody else separating me and Marquez. I remember blubbering snot and blood and crying like a child. "No! No! Don't take him! I can't let go of him! He'll die! He'll die!"

I remember screaming until I was hoarse, but no one listened.

I tried to warn them, but Harper and one of the other guys in the platoon pulled us away to get us onto litters for transport. I remember Harper and Roberts whispering to me, trying to calm me down, trying to soothe me, trying to tell me it was going to be all right. I remember seeing, out of the corner of my eye, a figure in a black shroud striding south into the darkened palm grove.

I knew the figure wasn't leaving alone.

There was nothing I could do. There still isn't. Death never picks the wrong house or the wrong day to show up. When Death arrives, the decision is Final. All I can do is delay–just provide a brief stay on the inevitable execution.

Oh, I've got *knowledge.*

But I don't have any power.

David R. Dixon served as a U.S. Army armor officer in both the active and reserve components, and deployed to Iraq three times. He lives in Springfield, Virginia. His book The Damsel *is available from Kyanite Press.*

Left-Hearted

By Michael Lund
Second-Place Prose, 2016

It was not until his 70th birthday that Jackson learned his IVC (inferior vena cava) was on his left side–not the right, as it is for more than 99.5 percent of all people.

"Oh, my gosh," he exclaimed dramatically, bursting into the family room where his wife was reading her book club's latest selection. "I'm left-hearted!"

He didn't even know what he meant when he said it, but something must have been in the back of his mind connected to left-handedness (which, he'd heard, artistic people tend to be) or left-leaning (as if politics were genetic).

"What in the world are you talking about?" Rita asked, folding *All the Light We Cannot See* on a finger to keep her place.

"That aortic aneurysm scan I had last week," he explained. "It showed that this major blood vessel in the middle of my body is on the wrong side–the IVC. All the blood in your lower trunk, abdomen, the pelvis and legs is carried to the right atrium of the heart by this, I guess, giant tube."

"You do have one, though, don't you?"

He frowned. "The aorta is on the right side. For all normal people, the IVC is more or less in front of it. But my IVC is on the left side of my body, way the hell from where it's supposed to be, backasswards."

"Well, you've been that way for seven decades, and you seem to function just fine."

"How can you say that? All my circuits are crossed; I have been mis-wired since birth, before then, I guess. Who knows what this has done?"

As he said it, three incidents rose up in memory, moments when he'd felt such strong emotion that his heart pounded and he thought he might die. One occurred in war ("if the face had been reversed," the radio man had said); a second in courtship ("star-crossed lovers," he thought); and the third with a career change ("the road not taken").

"Well, you're wired to me now, have been, in fact, for 46-and-a-half years. Better not say that's not as it should be."

"Humph." He wheeled around and stepped into the kitchen. The dishwasher, running, would drown out any more negative comments from her. And he could get himself a beer.

It irritated him when Rita dismissed his concerns, especially if it involved his health, physical or mental. And he had concluded on the drive home from the clinic that his misplaced inferior vena cava had doomed him to a inferior fate. He stuck his head around the corner to assert, "If my stupid IVC had been on the right side, where it was supposed to be, my life would have taken a different course. I could have been famous–certainly wealthy. I bet even a hero."

Retreating to the kitchen, he muttered, "Damn straight, wealthy from windmills."

He went to the bar he'd modeled on the style of British pubs. He's seen on some late-night show that pub masters in the Old Country keep their casks in the cellar and draw beer up to the bar with a long handled pump. He held his own glass at a slant under the mouth of his pearl-handled pump, which was connected to a keg in his basement. He drew slowly to minimize the foam and then took a long drink. (A voice inside his head said, "I hope our esophagus is correctly positioned and attached to our stomach!")

"Rita," he called. "I'm heading to the garden."

After 20 years as a competent mechanical engineer, building water treatment plants and reservoirs, he'd had a chance to switch to a start-up company making turbines for the latest hi-tech windmills.

"Jackson, my man," his college buddy Quentin said, "this is the chance of a lifetime. We've bought the rights to put windmills on a hundred miles of Wichita Mountain ridges. We can generate enough electricity to power half the state of Oklahoma."

He and Quentin had gone to what was, in the 1960s, the University of Missouri at Rolla (formerly the School of Mines and Metallurgy), in their home town. Their families couldn't afford to send them anywhere else, but it was a fine science and technology school.

He told Quentin, "I've got great seniority at Hydraulic, Inc., a solid pension plan, good salary. Most of what I do now is channel paperwork to the right places–smooth and easy is the flow. Haven't been out in the field in almost five years."

"Come out and see our prototype, Jack. Your heart will go pit-a-pat."

The Molino Gigante did, in fact, make his pulse flutter. The machine was a remarkable piece of workmanship, made out of remarkably strong but lightweight materials. It could withstand hurricane-strength winds, and its sealed and permanently lubricated parts would need almost no upkeep. Only a tornado right on top of one would do any damage.

But standing out on the isolated hilltop, Jackson had a panic attack. It was not just about starting life all over again. He'd have to ask his family to leave the only home they'd known. They would all need to learn the neighborhoods in a new town, find a home, transfer money to other banks, switch church and civic memberships to unfamiliar organizations, hand over their bodies to new doctors.

There was also something in that forbidding landscape—stark red rock, scrub trees battling prairie winds, hot summer baking the dirt, cold winters freezing the living. Rita, the son and two daughters, wouldn't like it.

He had never been good at relocation himself, suffering from homesickness at college and an almost complete disorientation when he went into the Army. His heart pounded, and he told Quentin no even as he admitted that the prospect was intoxicating. But his breathing was shallow from fear, not excitement. The firm took off, and he could have retired a wealthy man at 50.

If he hadn't been left-hearted.

He was comfortable in retirement but still worried by a gradual erosion of his assets. So he lived frugally, shopping for bargains and putting up vegetables he grew himself.

When he retired five years earlier, he installed an elaborate irrigation system in his backyard using two rain barrels fed by house gutters. Now all he had to do was turn the faucet and a steady flow would soak beans, tomatoes, squash, peppers, and eggplants all night long. He loved to watch the ground grow dark over the buried hoses with no charge to his water bill. He could imagine the plants' roots wicking moisture up to green leaves and ripening fruit.

"Dinner in 30 minutes." Rita had opened the kitchen window and called out to him. "Don't get involved in something."

Jackson thought of explaining that, like being left-hearted, his auditory system was probably crisscrossed. So what he heard was, "Do whatever you want, darling. You and I can dance naked to Duke

23

Ellington tunes and sip martinis all evening." But he raised a hand to acknowledge that he understood and said, "So long as my left-sided IVC doesn't make me veer off to another house and another stern housewife."

Contemplating his orderly garden–its hilled rows, tall tomatoes cages, pole bean teepees–he recalled the girl who got away. It was before he even knew Rita, which was after he came back from Vietnam. In college, he'd met one of the few female students in this engineering school and was love-struck.

Charlene Waters, a St. Louis girl, was posting the highest scores in an advanced mining engineering course. And she was ridiculously good-looking: cascading blonde hair, crystal blue eyes, and a slim, athletic body that slid into classrooms, seats, clothes. Jackson had never seen anyone like her and was determined to have his way with her. And so was every other unattached male at UMR.

They all quickly learned that Charlene could elude any attention she didn't desire. Still, Jackson channeled his energy into a single, brilliant (he thought) scheme to sweep her off her feet. He would show her the mine he and two of his childhood friends had dug into the bottom of a limestone cave just west of town.

"That independent project Professor Wells told us to complete?" he whispered to her before class began one day.

"Yes," she said with a noncommittal smile.

"I know where you and I could install a one-tenth-scale mine elevator that would go down into soft Missouri rock. We lower a grabbing mechanism–like what you see in those bowling alley claw machines–and see what kind of rock or whatever we bring up."

Another smile and a question. "When can we go check it out?"

This was too easy, he thought, but proposed they meet after Friday's class.

On the half-a-mile hike out he had to control his breathing as he watched her glide among the hickory and oak, dance across creeks on rock stepping stones, slip into the hillside cave as if she'd made this trip a dozen times. A model student, he thought, she was also a forest creature in her natural habitat.

The flickering flame of his kerosene lantern lit up the damp rock walls and ceiling. Jackson pointed out the eight-inch hole he, Bill, and Jody had bored through the floor. They'd linked together sections of metal pipe, jammed an old boat propeller in the end, and cranked it with a car jack wrench until they broke through to an underground cavity of undetermined size. It was one of those silly childhood projects he now hoped to turn into a young-adult romantic adventure.

"Listen," he said, dropping a pebble into the opening. In a second they could hear a distant plunk or splash. "That could be gold ... or oil."

"Or uranium," she said, kneeling beside him. "This is absolutely amazing. I'll build the grappling jaws and a wench system to send it down. We'll take pictures with my polaroid and get an A for sure."

"Let's use my 35-millimeter Nikon," he said. "It's a hobby, and I think we can lower it into our mine–take shots every foot down as we go."

Again, Jackson wondered at how smoothly this was going. His heart was racing when on the walk back he said, "Why don't we get a burger or something tomorrow? Go over the designs. You could come back to my house. I have a room in the basement."

Again, a lovely smile. "I'd like that." She stood up. "Of course, you *do* know I'm married." He felt the sound had just been sucked out of the woods, all air from his lungs.

They did carry out the experiment, got As on the assignment and in the course. She squeezed his arm when the grades were posted and said, "I wish I'd met you earlier. We're quite the team."

He now knew it wasn't bad timing that kept him from winning Charlene Waters (who became an astronaut and then manager of major NASA programs)–it was his left-heartedness. As a senior he had decided to take a year off after graduation and work for the National Park Service in Yellowstone. He got to see Old Faithful hundreds of times, but started college one year after Charlene, who met and married a plodding but pleasant geology major. Jackson's left-heartedness had made him leave when he should have stayed.

"Dinner in 10 minutes," Rita called from the kitchen.

Not that he didn't appreciate his wife. Still, it was unlikely she'd listen to Duke Ellington, dance naked, and sip martinis with him all evening as he imagined Charlene doing. He had three wonderful children and was generally content with his family. But ...

He'd always believed Vietnam had been a detour worse than Yellowstone. Many of his friends enlisted to get training and assignment for specific jobs in the military, but it must have been his left-heartedness that waited for the draft and insisted he go wherever the Army sent him.

During his induction he told the personnel specialist in charge of assessing his skills that he'd had his own darkroom since he was 12 and that his work had been in shows in high school. He loved developing his own prints, learning by experimentation how to vary times in the developer, stop baths, and fixers that bring out or suppress colors. The Army declared him a photographer.

It was a fine, if generally routine, military job: taking "grip and grin" photographs of promotions, awards, and other events. But one time, his Military Occupational Speciality put him in harm's way. Now he wonders if his imbalanced physiology might account for at least part of the terror that ambushed him.

"You *do* have balls, don't you?" his fellow photo specialist, Samuel ("The Sam") Pool, taunted as they rolled a die to see which one of them would go out with a squad setting up a night ambush. Ninety-five percent of their duties were on their huge base protected by overwhelming firepower; neither wanted this assignment.

"Well, small ones, of course," Jackson had countered. "Whereas yours ... still up in your abdomen."

The roll of the dice rolled Jackson out to the bush with a small group of battle-hardened soldiers. They must have read the fear on his face because they constantly reassured him. They knew what they were up to; it was unlikely they would encounter the enemy; the commanding officer was primarily staging operations to keep the brass off their backs.

"The VC know we're out here, man, and stay away from this route," explained Bob, the diminutive radio man. He pointed at a creased map of infiltration trails and the major roads in the area. "You stay back with me, set up your equipment, do what I do." You couldn't film night operations, but Jackson's commander wanted an authentic soundtrack for some unspecific future project. Jackson carried two portable tape recorders but also, just in case, a 35-millimeter camera.

The squad leader explained the Claymore mine defense they were putting around their position at dusk. "These babes rip through whatever's out there–man, tree, animal." He was placing green plastic cases on short legs just off the ground, each with a convex face. On the top were the words, "Front Toward Enemy." When the device was detonated, a layer of C-4 explosive blew about 700 steel balls in an arc that could be deadly up to 50 meters away.

"We're going to hunker back here, pay close attention to our listening devices, use our night vision goggles. If anything happens–and it probably won't–it'll be over in a millisecond."

His calming words were later offset by one man, probably irritated that they were saddled with a green correspondent. "Damn!" he whispered in Jackson's ear. "Hope I set that somma-bitch up facing the right way."

At a pre-dawn rustle of brush beyond their perimeter, Jackson felt his scrotum tighten. Then, when the flares lit up and the mines went off, there was a rush in his lower abdomen. The radio man later slipped him a clean pair of underwear.

Simple cowardice, Jackson had concluded and over time learned to live with the painful memory. Now it occurred to him that his system not his valor might have failed him. His vas deferens, the path his sperm was meant to travel on the way from testicle to urethra, had probably been misaligned since puberty, his ability to be a man twisted by biology, not mental or emotional weakness. Fear had taken over because his defenses were reversed, his capacities rerouted. Left-hearted.

"Dinner," called Rita. He sighed and went in, stopping to draw a second beer. "Feeling better?" she asked him at the table.

"I don't know. Still unsettled. Remember how, when our children asked our advice about what to study in college, and I always said, 'Follow your heart?'"

"I do."

"Well, I just wonder if I–or, more specifically, my congenitally misaligned circulatory system–channeled my own desires away from a higher destiny." He waved a hand at the room, the house. "All this is fine, of course, but perhaps I could have done more, done better."

Rita put down her fork. "Remember when your Army friend,'The

Sam' Pool, came that time ... what, 20 years ago?"

"Sure."

"Well, he told me a bit more about your night ambush story–which," she pointed a finger at him, "I was glad not to know about until 15 years after the fact. He said you rigged the dice so you would lose. He was married, had less than a month to go, so you took the assignment. I think your funny heart did right."

He looked down. "That's his story."

"And your turning down the Oklahoma job, which you say was your one chance to make it big? Part of the reason was that you didn't like the area, true. And you had your concerns about whether people would actually accept wind power. But you also knew we didn't want to move. The kids were happy in their schools. I had started work at the hospital. The family was happy where we were."

"Yeah," he admitted. "But ... "

"Don't even start on Charlene Waters! She wouldn't have kept you any longer than any of the four husbands and however many lovers she's had over the years! Your silly heart, however it's put together behind your bony old chest, took you right where you're supposed to."

He smiled.

"And," she concluded, "you look at some of the pictures of Miss NASA today and then you look at me." She sat up straight in her chair and tossed her hair. "Who would you rather be listening to 'Satin Doll,' sipping martinis, and dancing naked with until the wee hours of the morning?"

"You had me," he laughed, "at 'listening.'"

A native of Rolla, Missouri, Michael Lund is the author of numerous scholarly publications on the Victorian novel, two collections of short stories–How to Not Tell a War Story *and* Eating With Veterans–*and a number of novels inspired by The Mother Road, including* Route 66 to Vietnam: A Draftee's Story *(2004) and* Growing up on Route 66 *(1999). Professor emeritus of English at Longwood University, Farmville, Virginia, he conducts writing workshops for Home and Abroad, a no-cost writing instruction for military veterans, service members, and families.*

Bagging it Up

By Scott Hubbartt
Third-Place Prose, 2016

It was always blistering hot and that afternoon was no different. The exhaust of the idling plane's engines only made it worse, so the sergeant was silently grateful when the crew shut down the last spinning turboprop. White powder-like dust, kicked up when it taxied in, was just beginning to settle over the aircraft, and everything else, adding to the overall drabness of the remote airfield. He met the loadmaster at the back ramp and over the whining power unit called to him, "You're early. How many pax?"

"Thirty-two ... well, twenty-nine. Three didn't make it."

"All right. The medics are enroute. What's that guy's story?" he asked pointing to the litter being carried off and away to the shade of the aircraft's wing.

"Fucker stinks. Really bad."

"Hell, they all stink."

"No. This guy's really bad. Rotting."

The sergeant cocked his head at that and the loadmaster pointed to a guy in plain fatigues following the stretcher-bearers.

"Talk to him. The interpreter. He'll fill you in," pointing to a guy standing away from the litter patient.

"OK. I'll get on the horn and get the mortuary guys out here most skosh."

As he approached the Semitic looking guy in the unmarked fatigues he noted the U.S. flag sewn on his soldier and a 'INTERPRETER' strip sewn above his pocket. His name, 'ABDUL-AZIZ' was sewn over the over the other pocket.

"What's his story?" he asked as a way of greeting and pointed to the litter patient laying alone on the tarmac.

"Shit. I didn't think he'd last this long. See that bag he holding?"

"Yeah, what gives?"

"... his leg. Fucker's been hugging it since we picked him up day'n a half ago. Won't give it up. He was walking south, hands up, weapon slung upside down just like instructed, when about a hundred meters from the friendlies he finds a mine. Blew his fucking leg off. Took two of his buddies out. A corpsman stopped the bleeding but the guy wouldn't stop screaming until some grunt bagged his leg up and gave it to him. I guess this joker believes he can't go meet Allah without it. Thinks he wouldn't be whole. Thing is, it really stinks ... but he won't let go of it. The crew and the other POWs were complaining so we off loaded him."

Abdul-Aziz lit up a cigarette and offered another to the sergeant. Even though he didn't smoke he took it and lit it hoping to drown out the some of the stench which draped over them. Wondering which was worse, the putrid smell of the dying Iraqi or the sun's blistering heat, he debated walking away from the shade of the plane's wing but didn't. Instead he approached the dirty, whiskered, litter-borne prisoner and offered him his cigarette which he accepted with his free hand. He nodded his head gratefully and smiled up at the sergeant through yellow and missing teeth. For the first time he saw the mottled gray-green lump in the milky bag the guy hugged to his chest with his other bandaged arm. The acrid smell almost burned his nostrils so nodded to the guy and backed away.

Back with the interpreter, he asked him, "You a Moslim?"

"Yeah. But I was born and raised in Michigan."

"What do you think ... will he get into heaven with only one leg?"

"Well, if he does, I hope we can't smell anything up there." Then taking a long drag from his cigarette and handing what was left to the sergeant, he continued, shaking his head, "Fucker really stinks."

Scott Hubbartt enlisted in the U.S. Air Force at the age of 17, and later became a decorated combat veteran who rose to the highest enlisted rank. Hubbartt is a graduate of the Air Force's Survival, Evasion, Resistance and Escape (SERE) School and the U.S. Navy Senior Enlisted Academy at Newport, Rhode Island. Hubbartt wrote the 2014 survival memoir A Short Walk to the Edge of Life, *about facing dehydration, hunger, and exhaustion during a treacherous backcountry trek in the Peruvian Andes. He also holds a graduate degree in history and Latin American studies from American Public University. Hubbartt and his wife, Carolina, a native of Peru, have three daughters and live near San Antonio, Texas.*

The Stars and Stripes is Free

By Eric Chandler
First-Place Poetry, 2016

The *Stars and Stripes* is free.
I grab one to read
while I eat my eggs.
They're okay but the
bacon's not quite right.

A girl's face filled with glee.
The photo on this
page is black and white.
Her mom says this is
a party for her.

She is about to see.
The next picture shows
tears where the smiles were.
I stop chewing my
breakfast and lean back.

She fights to break free.
Her mother holds her
down inside some shack.
The other woman
dives in with a knife.

Why won't they let her be?
Why are the black robes
threatening her life?
The Kurd women cut
off some private skin.

I sip my hot coffee.
The Kurds are my team
in this war I'm in.

I see my own girl
getting blood, not cake.

It's hard for me to see.
A lie so awful
it makes my heart break.
To see daughters bleed
while I eat my eggs.

Eric "Shmo" Chandler is a husband, father, and pilot who cross-country skis as fast as he can in Northern Minnesota. His poetry collection Hugging This Rock: Poems of Earth & Sky, Love & War *was published in 2017. He is also the author of a collection of outdoor essays called* Outside Duluth, *and a novella titled* Down In It. *His writing has appeared in* Northern Wilds, Grey Sparrow Journal, The Talking Stick, Flying Magazine, Sleet Magazine, O-Dark-Thirty, *and* Aqueous, *as well as others. He is a member of Lake Superior Writers, the Outdoor Writers Association of America, and the Military Writers Guild. Chandler is also a veteran of both the U.S. Air Force and the Minnesota Air National Guard. He flew 145 combat missions and more than 3,000 hours in the F-16. He served in Iraq and Afghanistan. He enjoys cross-country ski racing and marathon running. He lives with his wife and two children in Duluth, Minnesota.*

Starling Wire

By David S. Pointer
Second-Place Poetry, 2016

What if the windshield of war and peace
were a glass eye: blue, green, brown,
laser red,
no matter,
invisible flamboyant mirages
becoming more vivid
microscopicesque
across the pagelessness, atop conflict ash
not
sprawling
on
un-airconditioned anti-social constructions
or retro-futuristically fitted, and refitted
for a carbon fiber marathon adventure run
through vast crematoriums inside craniums,
mortuaries, until starling wire swung down

David S. Pointer is the son of a piano-playing bank robber who died when David was 3 years old. He grew up in Kansas City and Clinton, Missouri. Pointer later served in the U.S. Marine Corps as a military policeman. He holds an undergraduate degree in criminal justice, and a graduate degree in sociology. His poetry has appeared widely in print and and on-line, in journals, anthologies, and chapbooks—the latter including such titles as Warhammer Piano Bar, Sinister Splashplay, Camelot Kid's Triggertopia, *and* Oncoming Crime Facts. *He currently lives in Murfreesboro, Tennessee.*

Culmination Point

By Jack Erwin
Third-Place Poetry, 2016

BAYONET X-RAY, BAYONET, X-RAY, THIS IS ACHILLES 22,
 OVER
GO AHEAD, OVER
DAILY REPORT FOLLOWS, OVER
SEND IT, OVER
LINE 1, RED
LINE 3, RED
LINE 5, RED
LINE 6, BLACK
LINE 9 BLACK, OVER
ROGER, GOOD COPY, CHARLIE MIKE, OVER
CHARLIE MIKE, OUT

RESTREPO 16, RESTREPO 16, THIS IS ACHILLES 22, OVER
RESTREPO 16, RESTREPO 16, THIS IS ACHILLES 22, OVER
RESTREPO 16, RESTREPO 16, THIS IS ACHILLES 22, OVER
THIS IS ACHILLES 22, NEGATIVE CONTACT, OUT
BAYONET X-RAY, THIS IS ACHILLES 22, OVER
THIS IS BAYONET X-RAY, GO AHEAD, OVER
ALAMO, OVER
ROGER, ALAMO, OVER

ACHILLES 22, ACHILLES 22, THIS IS BAYONET X-RAY, OVER
ACHILLES 22, ACHILLES 22, THIS IS BAYONET X-RAY, OVER
ACHILLES 22, ACHILLES 22, THIS IS BAYONET X-RAY, OVER
THIS IS BAYONET X-RAY, NEGATIVE CONTACT, OUT

Jack Erwin is a retired U.S. Army Field Artillery officer who served in Afghanistan, 2008-2009.

2017

Dirty Night Bingo

By Colin W. Sargent
First-Place Prose, 2017

"What's in this thing?" I shouted over the wop-wop of the Sea Knight's rotors. One hand on the stick, I held up the leather document case, glanced at its tearaway label. "Confidential." I shook it. In the black windscreen, the tower rose out of the darkness like a lighthouse.

"Dunno," Pete said. "NATO junk. None of our business. Let's just get this done and get back to the ship."

Looming 15 miles behind the desert island, the silver silhouette of the Arabian coast drew a line between the turquoise bathwater below us and the sea of sand ahead. I aimed our nose for the base of Masirah tower and dropped to a hover for one last run.

As the rotor brake stopped the wop of the blades, Pete unstrapped and turned back to Russell, who'd been staring at his unfamiliar .45.

"You know the drill," Pete said, pointing to the weapon. "No one comes close."

We walked briskly to the root of the tower. Pete stamped his hands in the cold. Thirty seconds after we hit the buzzer, the door lock buzzed back.

The elevator hummed us to the control floor. The door slid open.

"So, hell's freezing over?" Pete called in, but the genie whose bottle we'd invaded tapped his headset.

"You're Mister ... Arthur Lochried?" I asked.

He nodded, looking past my shoulder into the dark. "That's the Eisenhower out there, isn't it?"

We hadn't seen the Ike in days, even though we were part of her battle group.

"Yes, yes," he said, tapping his finger on his mike. "It's the Ike all right. I have them on Channel Five. They're 160 miles out. Lots of planes have launched. Listen."

Pete walked to the radio, the blinking status indicators. Behind us was a neatly made bed.

"Do you live here?" I asked.

"Yes, of course. I'll get some tea."

"You can desert the tower?"

COLIN W. SARGENT

"Yes! We're closed now! Look, I can turn out the runway lights!" He flipped a switch and the sky went blind.

"Magic," I said. "Just turn them back on when we leave."

He signed the receipt, then disappeared into the hall, pulling tomorrow out of the pouch.

Pete pulled up a squeaky metal swivel chair and put his feet up. The radio emitted drawls in the background.

"And Marshal, 501."

"501, Marshal."

"Make a recommendation to bring 502 down first, ah, because he'll be (garbled)."

"501, say again."

"Roger, this is 501, I would like 502 to come down first. Ah, once he's dirtied up, he's committed to a dirty Bingo."

"01, stand by."

"Hear that?" Pete was listening intently to the jets now, while I looked at the genie's personal effects. "That's his strike leader, trying to help him. They're going to bring him down first because he has a hydraulic failure. Young guy in an A-7, 'Moonraker 502.' He's low on fuel, 200 miles out. Once he drops his hook, gear, and flaps, he'll be 'dirty,' too–all that junk fixed in place below his jet like it was welded there. His fuel radius will be cut in half. They'll have to bring him right in."

"Mmm."

"501, unable, ah, 502 is last, sir."

"Roger that."

"Wow," Pete cooed in a low voice.

"What's up?" Arthur stuck his red and silver head into the room.

"A human sacrifice," I said, imagining myself behind the night dials.

Pete spoke with morbid excitement. "He's got a known hydraulic failure. I've just realized–CATCC is figuring there's a chance his hydraulics could fail on touchdown. His crash will wipe out the whole carrier deck for 20 minutes. Timing's too tight, with too many planes low on fuel. So they've got to land him last."

"Couldn't they just push his aircraft over the side?"

"Even that would take time. It's a war-at-sea strike. There are probably 70 planes in the air."

"501, ah, Marshal, how far out did you wish to dirty up?"

40

"I'd like about 15, please."

"And make that 20 if possible, Marshal, for 502."

"502, roger."

"Marshal, 502, could you get a squadron rep in CATCC, please?"

"502, say again."

"A squadron rep in CATCC."

"502, roger, stand by."

"What's your state, 502?"

"4.8."

"Say again."

"4.8, and I compute my dirty Bingo to be 4.1."

There was a pause. "Bingo divert 119 nautical miles."

I felt a chill. "Bingo"–the mystical point of no return, determined by fuel. A dirty Bingo cut that distance in half. With only 700 pounds of gas to spare, this kid was probably screwed to the moon.

"Thirsty?" Arthur walked behind a cloud of steam. Three cups and saucers were parked around a central English china pot adorned with a painting of an old farmhouse with a thatched roof. The place had a rugged door, a shepherd, and some pink- and lint-colored sheep. I turned around.

"You went to King's College?" I said, looking at an old graduation picture.

"Long time ago."

"How long you been here?"

"A million years."

"You're a sort of lighthouse-keeper here, aren't you?"

"There's more to this post than watching a Fresnel lens wheel round. I run the entire air base here."

"Don't you get lonely?" I pointed to a smoky picture of a blonde shaded by a weeping willow. "Who's that?"

He waved his hand, served me, then Pete.

Pete flicked off the carrier noises and spun his metal chair in our direction. "Our crewman's out there with our aircraft," Pete said. "We'll have to go soon."

"Did that lad land all right?"

"Last I heard he was told his Bingo divert was 119 miles out if he couldn't get on deck."

"Do you think he will make it to the carrier?"

Pete didn't say anything.

"There's a chance they'll send him here!" Arthur said. "I had better make some more tea."

By the time he returned, I'd divined Arthur was not precisely British, but the type of Canadian who ached to be British. Was that his crime? Was that why he was here? I looked involuntarily at the picture of the waved-off woman again.

"502 is three, well below glide path and on course."

"See? Your friend's coming in now," said Arthur. "Everyone's aware of his fuel state. They'll trap him right smart, using their arresting nets as a backup."

"Hey, I don't know this guy."

"502 is 2 miles, you're going, correction–centerline is slightly left, you're drifting right, you're holding well below glidepath, you're coming up now, slightly below."

"502 on glidepath and on course."

"502 is going slightly below glidepath, centerline is slightly right."

"502 is up and on glidepath."

"One mile."

"502, you are on glidepath, centerline slightly right, correcting, three-quarter mile, call the ball."

"502 Corsair, ball 4.2."

"Roger ball, Corsair, about 36 knots."

"Catch it."

"Power."

"Little power."

"Bolter, bolter."

"502, take angels 1.2, you're cleared downwind, report abeam, heading 180."

"502."

"502, your signal is Bingo, flaps up, hook up, climb passing angels 2, go button 14."

We looked at each other. He'd touched wheels on the Ike but missed the last wire, and we were his only chance now.

Arthur hurried into a chair and began transmitting into an ancient gray receiver. "Looks like we'll have company. He's coming here!"

"Pigeons 273/131."

I grimly smiled at the NATO codeword for course in degrees.

"One hundred thirty-one miles out," I said into the glass.

"502."

"Come to me," Arthur summoned from his screen.

"He's frozen stiff."

"Should we launch?" I asked.

"Negative, negative," said Arthur interrupting communications with the carrier. "I can't raise him, but I'm up with CATCC. They usually send along their H-3s in trail."

"Usually?" We stood up and looked through the floor-to-ceiling windows toward the ocean.

"I still can't reach him."

"Departure, Moonraker 502 on a Bingo."

"502, roger. I'm unable to raise flaps, ah."

"Roger."

"502, ah, rep."

"502."

"OK, did you turn the switch off, and, ah, your flaps are in the ISO position?"

"Affirm."

"They didn't come up at all?"

"Negative."

"Roger that, climb to 25 grand and, ah, start your dirty idle descent out about 35 miles."

"Ah, roger."

"And it's a trap on the long runway. If you miss the trap, you'll probably have about 1,200 pounds of gravy when you get there."

"Roger."

"Come to me," Arthur said.

"Still no joy?" we asked.

Arthur shook his head. "But it doesn't matter. Our navaids are up. Help me with these lights." He motioned to two large switches, each of which weighed as much as a flaming birch sidechair. I vomped them both to the "on" position and saw the blue taxiways remember their color slowly, then leap to full brightness. We waited.

"Why isn't is he talking to us?"

"I don't know."

"But it's been 10 minutes. Why isn't he in touch with the carrier?"

Arthur jumped up, pointed down. "I don't know. There he is!"

"He's 70 miles out." We saw the light, a single cell stirred up on Arthur's black radar wok, rocketing toward us.

"502."

"He's losing it," said Pete. "He's just saying his call sign."

"502, rep, say your state."

"Angels 19.5, 1.8."

A paralyzing silence. Then the rep's voice. "502, you don't have enough gas to get to your divert airfield." The words froze down the length of my spine.

We could not hear 502 transmit in reply.

"Help him!" shouted Arthur, and he started flashing the lights of the entire base off and on, on and off, vomp, vomp, a giant, 3-mile signal. We pumped the runway lights off and on like well water while I said, "Where'd all his gas go? I thought he had 1,200 extra pounds."

"It's his fault," said Pete. "He could have used his TACAN for a time and distance check against groundspeed. He could have called up the field on Data 89. They've got everything in those things now. He's got a heads-up display in there, you know."

"Yeah, Pete, it's all his fault."

"He's going to make it!" Arthur jumped between us.

The Corsair was coming in over the waves, burning too much gas even while losing altitude. Dirty. He called field-in-sight in the blind. Arthur activated the arresting gear and transmitted landing instructions.

"He's 2 miles from the numbers, approaching at 125 knots!"

Relieved, our host broke into a smile. The Corsair turned to a modified base leg for a landing on Runway 22, flying in a mineshaft but flying smooth, and descended to 700 feet. Then it made a funny hesitation, reduced airspeed, and turned parallel to the beach.

"Oh no–no, no!" Arthur was interrupted by the pilot's Mayday call. A couple of chugs later, he punched out. We saw the flash of his rocket-assisted easy chair directly over the waves and watched in disbelief as the Corsair sparkled into the shoreline like a discarded cigarette lighter.

"Bugs at a lightbulb." Arthur did a little dance. With sweetness the chute opened–with lazy, full, Louisiana pregnant sweetness. "I'm just a lighthouse, with all these ships hitting the ledge."

The pilot was awash in light now, the slow vowels of moonlight, runway lights, the open reflected night brilliance of the waves. We watched his feet, his legs, his black silhouette descend in the surf while screaming silly efficiencies at each other: "Shouldn't we launch?" and "No, they're sending the H-3s." "Move." "Now." "Look!"

Like that. Hornet talk. Even Einstein is inarticulate when a hornet is stinging him.

The chute collapsed into the nightmare surf. Light was cheap, everywhere. Arthur had thrown all Canada into the sky so that when we saw a black figure walking out of the blinding surf dragging a helmet in the water, he was backlit like some jerk blocking a drive-in movie picture on his way to the snack bar.

Shapes of humans—criminals—rushed to the waves before stepping respectfully to each side of him, forming a stony line as he approached, sideboys in a bizarre ceremony. Then the two H-3s appeared, giant angels with their landing lights on. Their rotorwash blew down on the pilot's wet parachute, beat it down in the night.

"They're taking him?" I asked. "Can't we do anything? He's trying to walk to us."

Arthur and Pete weren't talkative.

"Seriously?"

I ran for the door, bolted down the stairs, and blasted across the dizzy-hot tarmac toward the crashing waves. I ran closer toward the figure but then stopped 20 feet away. He'd taken off his helmet and as he focused on me I realized he looked exactly like me, from his sweep of dark hair to the malignant beginnings of a beard. I was suddenly so thirsty. The back of my throat became a desert. Suddenly that tea seemed like a good idea. I rubbed my eyes and tried to focus on the darkness ahead as I watched myself being led off for the debrief. In a typhoon of light and sound, the helicopters swept him away and disappeared into the sky.

Colin W. Sargent teaches writing at The College of William and Mary. A former CH-46D pilot and editor of the U.S. Navy's Approach *magazine, he started* Portland Monthly *in his home town of Portland, Maine in 1986, where he continues as editor and publisher. A Maine Individual Artist Fellow in poetry, and a graduate of the U.S. Naval Academy, he has a doctorate degree in creative writing from Lancaster University. His first novel,* Museum of Human Beings, *was published in 2008. His second,*

The Boston Castrato, *was published in 2016. He lives with his wife, Nancy, herself a former U.S. Navy officer, in Virginia and Maine. For more information, visit: www.colinwsargent.com.*

Walking Point

By Dewaine Farria
Second-Place Prose, 2017

Antoine, Oklahoma
September 1996

Hopped up on a cocktail of Quaaludes and speed, Sergeant Willie Kearns stormed into the mess hall and murdered three white soldiers. Then Kearns slumped to his knees, braced his rifle's stock on the floor, and pressed the warm muzzle into the flesh under his chin.

That's how I always pictured it anyway, so that's what I told the boys.

It was a bright, apple-crisp Sunday morning. The garage door was at half-mast, and a few autumn leaves had gathered on my gym mats.

I dug my hands into my kangaroo pocket and took a breath, turning from Simon's hungry stare to my own sons, Michael and Gabriel. I exhaled hard, while my sons' eyes remained fixed on Simon, waiting for his reaction.

All business, Simon strode to the chalk bucket in the corner of the garage, scooped up a handful and clapped a puff into the autumn air. One-hundred-and-eighty gymnast-lean pounds of unimpressed 16-year-old.

I twisted down the volume on whatever hip-hop foolishness them boys had going and tried to describe how the way-too-close-gunfire pierced the game of bid whist we had going at the rear camp in An Khe that day.

Crack-Crack-Crack. Pause. Then one more. *Crack.*

All the do-ragged heads bowed around my footlocker popped to alert. My boy Dawk called it.

"That's an M16."

I dropped my cards and rushed to the row of Quonset huts along with everyone else. The soldiers Kearns spared–two brothers and an esé–tottered into a clutch with the rest of us, watching the medics cart out three blood-soaked heaps of jungle fatigues on stretchers. Kearns they brought out last–doped to the eyeballs, endotracheal tube taped like a flagpole to the sloppy mass that had been his face, body still quaking in the Dexatrine funky-chicken. What is it about certain sons of bitches that makes them so got-damn hard to kill?

"That's it?" Simon asked.

I'd left out the part about sons of bitches, but studying Simon's restless, oil-slick dark face, I understood that including that tidbit wouldn't have made any difference.

Michael spoke up. "Not quite the brothers-in-arms shtick you were hoping for, huh, Sy?"

I jerked a thumb at the two 45-pound plates on my side of the barbell. "You good with this, Sy?"

"Yeah, leave it, Mr. Frank," Simon answered, a little quicker than he outghta have.

Simon had been my eldest son Michael's best friend for something like five years by then. A near-permanent fixture at my house. He shoulda known he wasn't getting some foxhole brotherhood bullshit outta me.

"I ever tell you guys I had to get circumcised after I was drafted?"

"How old were you?" Gabriel asked. My youngest, the writer. Well, he was still dancing back in the fall of '96. That'd put him at about 12.

I scissored my fingers in Gabe's direction. "Just turned 18."

That set the three of them to squirming in their sneakers, hands inching towards nether regions.

"So, circumcision was a condition of your conscription to fight a war for a government that treated you like a second-class citizen?" Michael asked, without pausing for breath.

I chuckled. "Exactly." Over the years I'd referred to getting drafted as a lot of things–mostly as a motherfucker. Never as conscription.

"The unkindest cut of all," Michael said, shaking his head.

"Julius Caesar." Simon flashed them pearls at Michael. I think I remember every time I saw that boy smile. He was stingy with his grins, like each one cost him 50 bucks and he was on a limited income.

"A'right." I tapped my hand on the barbell. "Enough messing around, Sy. Let's go."

Simon slid under the weight, settling his shoulders onto the bench's leather cushion. He clasped and unclasped his fingers on the perforated steel, then pulled himself eye to barbell and lowered himself back to the bench. Once. Twice. On the third go he popped the weight off the rack with his funky "oohyuhken" grunt–from that *Street Fighter* video game them boys loved so much. Simon lowered the bar to his chest then fought it back up. Steady. Machine-like. For a solid set of eight. Two more than I'd got. I guess that Vietnam hair the boy had had up his ass all morning was good for something.

"Oh, I see you angling for a title shot, huh, young blood?" I said, twisting my trunk in an exaggerated torso stretch.

All three laughed at that.

As a deputy warden over at Antoine State Prison I hadn't done a forced cell movement in more'n a decade, but I still pushed heavy weights. Or at least tried to. Simon—a three-sport jock, who'd left us hoarse from cheering after his 11 catches for a hundred and seventy-eight yards against Tecumseh last week—had been matching me plate for plate for more than a year by then.

I pointed at Michael's and Gabriel's smirks. "Can either of y'all push that for eight?"

Gabriel piped up, "Mom named us for angels, Dad, not dwarves. You know dwarves get a ..."

"A bonus on their strength score," I interrupted.

Michael and Gabe had my caramel complexion and good looks, but not my stocky frame. They used that dwarf joke on me a lot. I didn't mind. Besides, them two brainiacs preferred my Sunday morning gospel of steel to the fire and brimstone they got every time their mother dragged them down to New Hope Baptist.

"Hold up. Hold up," Simon said, leaning over his knees on the bench and pointing at the stereo. "Turn up that Tupac joint."

Michael obeyed, and all three listened in silence to what sounded to me like an X-rated Saturday morning cartoon jingle. Tupac. That boy with all them frivolous tattoos. Like an affair, ink is something a man should only do if it really means something.

"This guy getting shot is a big deal, huh?" I said, indicating with my fingers for Michael to lower the volume a bit.

Michael twisted the knob, plopped cross-legged next to the stereo on the cobalt-grey gym mat, and looked up at me. "Do you remember when Marvin Gaye died, Dad?"

"Vaguely."

"Well, I remember it. You were washing the car. Mom came running outside with the news. You said, 'Jesus,' then sat on the curb."

"How old were you then?" I asked, starting the math in my head.

Michael blinked twice. "Five. But I remember. You sat there awhile."

I grunted and restrained my smile as Michael turned the volume back up. What would I have done with my life if I'd had half them boys' brains?

Sy bounced from the bench to his feet. He leaned over, touched his toes–chest pressed to his thighs–and held. Tough, smart, and strong that one. If somebody had dealt me that boy's hand, I woulda thrown mine in.

I sure as shit wouldn't have enlisted. That's for got-damn sure.

At work the next Saturday, Ettie sat on the opposite end of my tan metal desk watching me thumb through her "Prison Rape Elimination Plan."

"You know what the COs are saying about this PREP stuff, right?"

"I can guess," Ettie said.

"Install liquid soap dispensers in the showers."

Ettie, perched like some kinda Ethiopian goddess in my burnt-orange carpeted office, looked at me.

"You know." I met her gaze for the punch line. "That way no one can drop the soap."

Ettie, unsmiling, tucked a braid behind her ear. "That's actually pretty good."

I hadn't cracked that PREP folder all week. She could definitely tell.

"Did you speak to Simon?" Ettie asked.

Something else I hadn't done.

"Yeah." I paused. "Kind of."

"What's that mean?"

"Means I think the boy has his mind made up regardless of what I tell him."

"Did he tell you," Ettie asked in that cadence black women reserve for speaking to trifling motherfuckers, "that his father died on Tuesday?"

I musta seen Sy half a dozen times since our weightlifting session last weekend. He hadn't said a thing. Jesus. Sixteen years old and that boy carried himself like Jim Brown in the fourth quarter.

"I've never talked to Simon about his father. He never brought him up. Besides, I didn't want to give the impression I was trying to take his dad's place."

"News flash, Frank." Ettie waited for me to meet her eyes. "You filled that void a long time ago."

"You said Simon never met him. His father, I mean."

"Never. And now he's gone, same as Simon's grandfather."

Ettie had a prison marriage followed by a prison divorce. It's a lot more common than people think. She had already been counseling at Antoine for a few years when I started there in '76, a year after I got my DD-214. Now she ran counseling programs for the whole state, which meant that sometimes–like today–she worked Saturday evenings too.

I pinched the ridge of my nose. "Troy, right?"

Ettie nodded.

Actually, I'd had no trouble at all remembering the name. Troy. The guy Ettie had constantly been shuttling back and forth from California to see back when I was still single. I'd looked at Ettie differently back then, but nothing had ever came of it. And now I have a managerial job, a wife, a family; I loved the last two, didn't hate the first. More than all that though, I depended on Ettie mentoring my boys. Hell. Michael had been in junior high when Claire and I gave up on trying to keep up with his reading.

"We'll be going down to New Orleans for the funeral. Simon will meet some of his father's ..." Ettie scanned the off-white stucco wall behind me before deciding on "colleagues."

"Panthers?" I asked.

"*Former* Panthers." She smiled tightly. "I talked to Claire a couple hours ago."

Ettie was pulling out all the stops; she knew full well that, even after all these years, my wife had never fully warmed to her. Claire the red-boned, processed-hair, we-shall-overcome church girl and Ettie the headwrap-wearing, Angela Davis-spouting ideologue who wasn't passing anybody's paper-bag test. Claire had accepted Ettie like she did my night shifts: something you tolerated for decent health insurance. And Ettie knew it.

But Simon–calloused as he was to the world–never failed to make Claire laugh, probably more than she wanted. And Ettie knew that, too.

"Claire and I agreed that you need to talk to Simon before we head down to New Orleans. He's on the cusp, Frank. Him and Michael. They'll be 17 in a couple weeks. Old enough for the military's delayed-entry program. The decisions those two make this year are biggies."

"I don't think Michael is too interested in the military."

Ettie laughed a little too loud at that. "You think?"

The boys did spend just about as much time at her house as they did at mine. Ettie was notorious for breaking up summertime Super Nintendo marathons with mandatory 30-minute reading breaks.

"I don't know what to tell that boy about the military. Even when I first got back, I never talked about Vietnam much. Lessens the chance of someone pissing me off."

That excuse sounded even more pathetic than the shit about not wanting to replace Simon's father. Everybody knows someone who'd fought in Vietnam and didn't want to talk about it. Still, I figure it's better than being one of those guys who never shut up about it, the ones who saw themselves as the true victims of the war. Everybody knows one of them guys too.

"Tell him the truth," Ettie said.

The prison's public announcement system screeched to life, startling both of us. "Code Red, Wing Two! Code Red, Wing Two!"

Ettie smoothed her pants against her thighs. "Should I wait in my office?"

Ettie and I had worked together in the Oklahoma Department of Corrections for more than 20 years. Long enough for her to know that—whether this was an assault on a correctional officer, a fight between inmates, or a medical emergency—as a counselor her role was, for now, to get outta the way.

I stood up behind my desk. "Give me an hour or so to sort this out." I tapped a finger on the PREP folder. "I know this is important. We'll discuss it, OK?"

Ettie's gaze dropped to her watch. I glanced at the wall-mounted clock behind her. 18:30 already.

"Let's do it Monday." Ettie stood.

"Don't make me have to track your sorry ass down again, Frank." She placed a hand on her hip. "Good to go?"

"Good to go." I repeated, smirking. "And I'll talk to Simon. Really talk to him."

I hauled-ass-for-leather down the stairs of the staff wing, across the reception area, and up to the thick glass of the control room. Measmer, a gangly, blond former coastguardsman fresh out of the academy, leaned into the VHF radio base station, pen poised over a blank notepad.

I drummed my fingers on the glass, caught the youngster's eyes, and pointed to the door.

"Oh shit. Sorry, Warden," Measmer mouthed. He walked to the 1950s-style control panel and buzzed me in.

"What do we got?" I asked.

"Not sure, Warden. Nestor's in charge in Wing Two today."

We exchanged a look. Measmer got it. A good kid. One of the best to come out of that class.

"None of them have gotten on the horn yet to confirm what's going on. Nothing on the CCTV either." Measmer gestured to the row of TV screens flickering between black and white views of empty stairways, hallways, and rec rooms.

"Try Nestor again," I said.

Measmer keyed the VHF handset. "Whiskey Tango One, this is Charlie Romeo."

The handheld on my hip squawked from proximity to the base station. I twisted the knob on the device to turn down the volume.

"Charlie Romeo, this is Whiskey Tango One." Nestor's voice, giddy with excitement, crackled through the VHF speaker. "Alert Delta Whiskey One that he needs to come up here."

Measmer looked at me.

"Tell him I'm coming up," I said.

Measmer spoke into the handset, "Copy that. Delta Whiskey One *en route*." Then to me, "Want me to go up with you, Warden?"

"What? And abandon your post?" I placed my hand on Measmer's shoulder. "Hold down the fort here."

Measmer buzzed me through to the prisoner side of the facility.

My corfams echoed in the deserted hallway, their glossy shine reflecting the dull glow of the wall mounted emergency lights–that dim 24-hour reminder of the reality of incarceration. I bounded up the ladder well to Wing Two and punched the buzzer, mind tight with that rush I learned to sorta love and sorta hate during the war.

Nestor swung open the steel door. Physically, he wasn't a punk. Nestor stood well over 6 feet and had proved on prisoners' bodies just how much of his bulk he could transform into brute force. But he was still a coward.

Nestor began speaking before I could even step in, his tone that of a tattling schoolboy. "Riggs threatened me from his cell. He's got a shank. Now he's demanding to talk to you." He waited a good five seconds before adding, "Warden."

I gave him a look that could have reshaped iron. "Let me in, Nestor."

Two standing fans oscillated hot air and the smell of disinfectant around the taut, windowless space. Eight COs suited in react gear–body armor, batons, and shields–stood rattling against each other in the area just before the cellblock, artificial light glinting off their lowered visors. Nestor cocked his head in anticipation of my orders.

If a cartoonist was to sketch a prison guard–exploiting every lame-ass stereotype us COs despise–he would turn out someone exactly like Nestor. The latest accusation of misconduct against the bastard involved instigating a fight between two inmates.

"Did you see those fucking apes going at it?" Nestor had joked in the break-room afterward.

Nestor never talked about the event that prompted his transfer from McAlester prison a few years ago. But I heard young COs whisper to one another, "That's him. That's Colin Nestor. Dude broke a con's jaw in Big Mac." Nestor loved that the story had grown legs.

The seasoned COs almost universally disliked Nestor, but they'd back him against a con. The same groupthink compelled soldiers to cover for each other in Vietnam, for everything from curfew violations to rape. But institutional loyalty alone didn't explain the concentrated aggression in front of the cellblock that day.

Behind their face shields the COs' eyes pleaded for a "go" order. They wanted to storm a cell and stomp a con. I know the feeling. Hell. I love that rush of fraternal adrenaline as much as the next guy. But nowadays, it was my job to ask questions; and when it came to the Nestors of the world, I had plenty.

"I saw the weapon," Nestor spoke more to the other COs than to me. "Reason enough for a forced cell move to Special Quarters." Long pause. "Warden."

"Shut up, Nestor." I turned to the assembled COs. "Stand fast here. Lemme try talking to him first."

"Roger that, Warden." The COs responded in unison.

I started down the row of cells, a spider of cold sweat crawling down my back. The cellblock reeked of that pitched battle between human excrement and industrial strength bleach. As a Deputy Warden, I didn't walk the rows much anymore. The stench I had grown used to while earning my stripes immediately set my heart to thudding in my chest nowadays.

A detached voice from behind the bars cursed all creation. "Fuck me. Fuck this. Fuck you."

My gut corded. "It's Warden Mathis, Riggs."

A shank clattered onto the grey tiled floor in front of the cell.

"'Preciate you coming up, Warden," Riggs said. "I know your boys out there are chomping at the bit for a go at me."

I kneeled, picked up the shank, flipped it around in my hand. A toothbrush handle reinforced with electrical tape, sharpened on the end, and spliced with a disposable razor. A nasty little piece of work. Prison and war encourage ingenuity.

I stepped in front of the cell. "What's going on, Riggs?"

Riggs leaned his forehead against the bars. "That bitch-ass Nestor talking about how the last governor granted less than 3 percent of paroles for lifers. Like I don't already fucking know that shit."

As a black, non-snitching, former gangbanger convicted of murder, Riggs occupied the top of the Antoine prisoner hierarchy—a delicate equilibrium of connection, conviction, sexual preference, and race (not necessarily in that order).

I'd known Riggs since I was a rookie CO. Back when I was still walking the yard during rec time, watching sparrows catch a buzz on the electric fence, knowing full well I was within swinging distance of every concealed shank on that patch of grass and concrete—the only part of Antoine that the sun touched. Hell, the better part of both our lives had been more about prison than anything else.

"You pulled the shank to get Nestor to shut up."

"Yeah," Riggs replied.

"You got anything else in there we need to know about?"

"Nah."

"You sure? You know my boys are fixing to turn this cell inside out."

"I'm sure, warden."

"Relax, Riggs." I slipped the shank into my cargo pocket. "They'll do their search and that'll be it. No one's going to pursue this. Try to get some sleep. We'll have the governor's decision in the morning."

Riggs nodded, opened his mouth as if to thank me, but instead squeezed his eyes shut and nodded again.

The governor's denial of Riggs' parole came through bright and early, just after first count.

I stayed on a couple hours after shift to escort Riggs back to Gen Pop myself. That, and to have a couple choice words with Nestor–if he tried to write up Riggs he'd be doing so without any support from me.

By the time I left the facility late Sunday morning all I wanted was to shit, shower, shave, and sleep.

Back at the house, after ticking the first two off my list, I wiped the steam from my bathroom mirror in preparation to enjoy the third. I squeezed a dime-sized portion of shaving cream onto my boar's-hair brush, then splayed the lather across my face to the sounds of Claire fussing over church clothes in our bedroom. I reached over my head with my left hand, pulled the cheek tight, and slid the razor along my face in short, smooth strokes. A proper shave. Ain't nothing quite like it.

If memory serves, it was later that same year that I demonstrated the process to the boys. When I flicked out my straight edge Simon looked me dead in the eyes, serious as a heart attack, and said, "That is so fucking bad-ass, Mr. Frank." Setting the four of us to giggling like schoolgirls.

I got my first proper shave at Am Tinh's, the spade whorehouses outside the base camp in An Khe. Back in '71, the G.I. version of tolerance didn't extend to getting laid. Shit. Probably still don't. The white boys hocus-pocused some of the Vietnamese whores into Sally-Annes and viciously protected their investment. Meanwhile, the fiercest black cats made sure that only down white boys set foot in Am Tinh's.

"Trust me, young blood," my best friend Dawk told me, running the saw edge of his Swiss Army knife through his moustache. "Joint's got the best juke box in 'Nam."

I chose Qui, a "mamma-san" in her, maybe, late twenties, which put her a decade ahead of me. Had myself half convinced that choosing Qui was some kind of enlightened decision on account of her age. Truth told, those teenage whores–with faces hardened by nights of straight liquor and closed fists–terrified me. 'Course, Qui frightened my 19-year-old-ass too, but she was older, and somehow that made the whole arrangement seem OK. It took getting home to realize just how unrecognizable my wartime caveats had rendered my morals. That's the thing: When you go to war, your soul is at as much hazard as your body. More really.

Still, I'd be lying if I didn't admit how much I savored those nights at Am Tinh's. The baths that never quite washed off the exhaustion and fear, the saffron-tinged breeze flapping the floor-length vanilla curtains, those deep purple and cotton-candy pink sunsets through the glassless windows, drifting off to sleep with Qui bent over me like a human orchid. And that's exactly how I'd treated her: Like an ornament. Her English was good, but I was having the first steady sex of my life and hadn't really been listening. Qui had mentioned a mother. A sister. A village.

"The people surrender to whoever is there. When the VC came, we surrendered. When the Americans came, we surrendered. If the NVA come, we surrender." Here Qui smiled, ran her hands through hair so black it stole the light. "That is how we survive."

In the mirror, I noticed Claire watching me.

"How long you been there?"

"Long enough to know your mind is someplace else." Claire raised a manicured eyebrow. "Ettie called last night."

"Man. She is in a full-court press."

"Can you blame her?"

I met Claire's gaze in the bathroom mirror. It took a lot for her to say that. All these years and Claire still manages to surprise me.

"The boys are down in the basement," Claire said. "All ready for you to get them out of morning service so y'all can lift."

"I'm gonna talk to them." I glided the straight-edge over my cheek. "All three of them."

Number four on my to-do list was gonna have to wait.

Claire nodded, watching her reflection as she adjusted the lace doily pinned to her hair.

"New church crown?" I winked, holding the blade under the tap.

Claire nudged her shoulder into my back. "This one I've had for years."

I headed to the couple bottles I kept tucked in the corner of the "good" living room, the showpiece that Claire never allowed any of us to actually sit in. I filled half a glass with Crown Royal then lifted it to my nose with both hands and let the scent warm my lungs. I topped off the glass with soda water. All them rules about drinking in the morning go out the window once you start working shifts. Hell. I deserved a drink before this conversation.

I caught up with the boys in my basement, watching BET.

"Hey, guys."

Simon, gave me a thumbs-up from his usual spot on the floor, head propped up on a sofa pillow. "Hey, Mr. Frank."

Michael and Gabriel nodded to me from the couch.

I lowered myself onto the recliner, setting my glass on the armrest and missing the days when sitting down didn't require so much effort.

"I want to talk to y'all about the Army."

Simon, cradling his knees between his elbows, rocked himself to a seated position.

"Come on." Michael tapped Gabriel's leg. "Let these two indulge their fascist side."

My sons stood up, and Simon made a play swipe at Michael's leg.

"No." I looked at my sons. "I want you two to stay."

Michael and Gabriel exchanged shrugs, then settled back onto the couch.

I took a breath.

"Most of the fighting I was involved in took place in Cambodia. That probably don't mean a whole hell of a lot to you guys now. But it meant we fought more NVA than Viet Cong. North Vietnamese regulars. Professionals. Real soldiers, like us.

"The heavy contact went down about 10 or 15 miles over the border. I can count those times on one hand. I was shitting myself with fear every time. I spent that entire year terrified and exhausted. Hell, sometimes the only reason I didn't make a run for it was because I was just too got-damned tired." I paused, looked at Simon. "You'd handle it better." I waved off his protest. "Nah. You would. But there was something else, too. Kind of like getting off. Like an orgasm, when you thought you smoked one."

That last bit was embarrassing. But how do you express it? That war is hell, but at its height, it's also life. Life multiplied by some number no one's heard of yet.

"Mostly we shot farm animals though. Pigs, chicken, oxen ..."

"Why?" Simon asked.

"Some villages were suspected of supporting the enemy. Hell, the only reason I carried my Zippo was to burn hooches. I didn't even smoke."

Fragile, ancient things, them villages. Without hardly putting our minds to it, we'd decimate even the big ones in a single afternoon. The whole company–a hundred plus grunts–watching flames take shape on thatched roofs in the midday sun. My 19-year-old mind figuring that surely this many people wouldn't expel this much effort on something wrong, would they?

Then the sergeants would form us up, and we'd drag-ass on. Flamethrower heat from them smoldering huts at our backs, women's screams ringing in our ears, usually without a single VC in tow, and me so fucking exhausted that, as far as judgment went, I might as well have been piss-drunk.

"What do you mean, 'when you thought you smoked one?'" Gabriel asked.

"You could never really be sure."

I didn't know shit from apple gravy when I first showed up. Under ambush, I aped the guys in my platoon and sent rounds downrange. *Ta-tat-tat-tat-tat-tat-tat.* Like the air was alive with lead. Looking back, I'm pretty sure something would have shifted inside me if I'd actually killed someone. I would've known. But I didn't tell the boys that. I didn't wanna cop outta what I might've done.

"My first squad leader was a lot like you, Simon. Dawkins. Terrell Dawkins. Tough motherfucker. All gas, no brakes. Always volunteering to walk point." I shook my head, smiled. "Sniper bait. When I first met him, I thought he was nuts."

I tried to describe Dawk during that first meeting. Sitting on a rock, face two hollow cheeks with a thick nugget of a nose in-between, flipping the selector switch on his weapon back and forth between semi and full while staring off into the bush like some crazy Zulu tribesman.

Take your average understrength infantry company–100 spics, spades, and white trash. Ten shouldn't be there. Eighty are just targets. Ten do the fighting and, if you're lucky, one of these is a got-damned savage. That was Dawk. In a cadre of touched men Dawk's mania stood out, making him the platoon superstar.

"Dawk's theory was that the second man was more likely to get hit than the first. The kind of guy who didn't get medals, just that deep field respect that mattered more." I stopped short, reminding myself: no bullshit. "He was a good killer. One of our best."

"'Fortune favors the bold,'" Simon said.

"'God smiles on idiots and drunks,'" Michael shot back.

"I don't know about all that." Those two. Constantly tossing quotes back and forth. "In war you learn more about cowardice than courage. That and luck."

All them crazy superstitious rituals to fool yourself into believing that it wasn't just random. Always volunteering for point. Only smoking on every second break. Never walking in tank tracks. Anything to convince yourself that getting smoked depended on more than just ending up fifth in line on patrol, or where you took a dump, or when you noticed that your bootlaces were untied. War didn't give a shit if you were loved by many or not at all. Charlie was greasing 300 GIs a month in '71, and every one of their mommas had told them they was special. A reality so fucked up that superstition became the only rational system of belief. It just so happened that Terrell's crazy-ass superstitious rituals gave that motherfucker the confidence to stalk the jungle like a got-damned immortal. Boys like Terrell–and Simon–don't need much convincing of their immortality. In my experience, that type fears cowardice more than anything that might actually kill them.

In the bush, Dawk spotted loose soil, crushed foliage, and catgut trip wires. He heard the unnatural silence before an ambush as if possessed of some deeper understanding of these people clawing for their survival. Still, on some level we all musta known that part of it was just dumb luck that kept us from getting hit when Terrell was on point. But the fact remained: the men of 3rd Platoon, Bravo Company didn't get hit when Dawk walked point. Never. Not once. Even on patrols a good 10, 15 miles into Cambodia. The heart of Indian Country. So far out that we was resupplied by mermite cans kicked out the side of a Huey.

"Dawk was already in his second tour when I showed up in the summer of '71. He had something to prove. Usually that made guys dangerous. But not Dawk. I think deep down, Dawk wanted to challenge all the things white boys had been telling him his whole life. He reveled in how them white boys feared, respected, and required his ferocity–out there in the bush, searching for something only he wanted to find. After he made staff sergeant, he bucked for a third tour. When my year in country was up, I rotated back to the States and spent the rest of my enlistment at Fort Hood handing out basketballs at the base gym."

I licked my lips and took a sip of my Crown and soda.

"Terrell and me used to talk a lot about Black Nationalism. How the war in Vietnam was going to change everything for the black man in the United States. He once asked me what niggers had done when they returned from America's other wars." The boys winced. I guess that word grated outta my mouth, but not Tupac's. I plowed ahead. "They'd kept on being niggers. But this time it was gonna be different."

When I was Simon and Michael's age, almost everyone I knew was black. Lieutenant Nic Voivodeanu, the 3rd platoon commander, had been my first white friend. Well, as much as a 2nd Lieutenant could be a PFC's friend anyway.

One time in the mess hall in An Khe, Nic spotted me in the middle of scratching out a letter home.

"Who're you writing to, Mathis?" Nic asked.

"My mom, sir."

I returned to my letter, but felt the LT still there, examining the top of my head.

"Sir?" I asked, looking up.

"How old are you, Mathis?"

"Nineteen, sir."

Nic grinned. "I bet your parents are proud."

I didn't say how, before leaving for Boot Camp, my mom made a point of telling me about the battered, castrated body of a black WWII veteran, swinging from a yellow poplar in her neighborhood back in Tennessee.

"They'd stripped off his uniform before stringing him up," my mom said. She talked about the racism of those days—the unrelenting terror of it all—without bitterness or self-pity. That's just the way things were.

Nah, I didn't tell my West Point-educated lieutenant that. Instead I nodded and returned the LT's smile. But you best believe I told my boys about that lynching. In the basement that day, I told them boys to love their country. It's the only one we got. You better love it, try to make it better. But don't ever get caught acting like it can't happen. It did. It does.

Nic couldn't understand the rage of the flip-flopped men tracking our platoon in the bush, still less those flip-flopped men's perfect comprehension of us black draftees marching for an empire that didn't want us. The same way a kid like Measmer couldn't see himself pulling a shank on someone like Nestor. They see gooks and cons, where I see men with identities shaped around survival. Men like me, only more desperate and maybe, just maybe, more brave.

"We arrived to Vietnam just two more boys unable to get out of that Selective Service letter." I knifed a hand in Michael's direction, unintentionally giving the boy a jump. "Conscripts. But we became volunteers. Every single one of us over there was really a volunteer."

That last bit I said more to myself than to the boys.

"The lieutenant wrote to me at Fort Hood when Dawk finally bought it."

I'm not sure how long it took to medevac Dawk back to the division hospital, after he stepped on that manure tinged punji stick. I do know that once the wound went gangrenous, Dawk was dead in a week. Staff sergeants didn't walk point. Maybe Dawk had been the number-two man when the contaminated wood pierced his boot. Nic didn't say.

I wasn't close to all the guys our platoon lost in Vietnam. I watched in silence as Pfc. Danny Pierce gurgled pink waiting for a dust-off. Doc Reynolds on his knees next to him, fighting all those obscene, animal bits leaking outta the hillbilly's punctured body. Exactly a week earlier, Nic had ordered Pierce to remove the Confederate flag he'd draped over his bunk. Nah, I hadn't felt sorrow while Pierce lay there, making the sound of a baby working up the energy for a good scream. Distress and disgust, yeah. Same as I'd felt when they'd carted Sgt. Kearns' psychotic black-ass outta the mess tent. But not sorrow.

But here's the thing. Losing so many contemporaries–boys like Dawk, Pierce, and Kearns; boys with similar hopes, fears, and families– so early in life wears on your soul in a way that I couldn't articulate. Hell. How do you articulate any of it? How napalm leaves less than bones? The violent beauty of muzzle flashes at night? Growing old in an afternoon? Friendships cleansed of all that shit that seems so important back in the world? How someone getting killed starts to feel natural. And why shouldn't it? Most of human existence had been closer to that, hadn't it?

Instead, I maintained an eye contact with Simon that the teenager–

as tough as that boy was–just couldn't bear.

"The things that defined my service won't define yours." My gaze settled onto my hands, clasped around my glass. "Kids join the military for a lot of different reasons, Sy. Make sure you're doing it for the right ones."

A week later, Simon attended his father's funeral in New Orleans. Two weeks after that, back in Antoine, I drove Simon to the recruiters' offices.

Ettie wasn't angry, or at least she didn't show me any anger. "He's made his decision," she told me on the phone when they were back from Louisiana. "I'm at peace with it. But you should be the one to drive him."

Throughout all this, Simon didn't mention his dad once. Still hasn't.

"What defined your service, Mr. Frank?" Simon asked as we drove to Antoine's storefront row of recruiting stations, bookmarked by a Piggly Wiggly grocery and a Blockbuster Video.

I stared at the station wagon's windshield for a couple seconds.

"Violence, race, and drugs."

"Those things won't define my service."

He was probably right. Them boys generally was.

We talked to all four. The Marines don't have special forces, the Army could guarantee a slot at Ranger School but nothing more, and Simon didn't like the Navy's uniforms. While walking between recruiting offices, Simon and I got a good laugh outta how Michael woulda responded to this less-than-scientific process of elimination. Simon ended up signing a delayed-entry contract with the Air Force that guaranteed him a shot at pararescue: "The PJ pipeline." Special Forces right outta the gate. Exactly what Simon wanted..

The boys graduated in the spring of '98 and had one last summer together. In the autumn, Michael packed for Columbia University, Simon for Lackland Air Force Base.

The governor granted Riggs' parole six years later. May 5, 2004. A Wednesday. Measmer, looking sharp and confident with supervisor's pips shining on his collar, walked Riggs downstairs. I watched Measmer and Riggs trading jokes as they passed through the sally port to the staff side. Measmer handed me the manila folder that contained Riggs' file. I signed the pink release slip paper-clipped to the front of the folder. Then I shook Riggs' hand. In my 27 years at Antoine, this was the third time I personally met a prisoner for release.

Riggs smiled, eyes wide and moist at the edges. "Now for the hard part."

I found Simon sitting in my living room with Ettie, Claire, and Gabriel that evening.

Simon, in ramrod straight civvies, popped to his feet when I walked in. "Look at you, old man."

I grabbed him and held him way too long in a vain attempt to chokehold the restlessness still pulsating from his body. Be still now, son. Now is the time to be still.

Simon told prepackaged, safe war-stories. The constipation from weeks of eating nothing but MREs, the Afghan interpreter who had a penchant for walking on his hands in the nude and whose English was flawless until he cussed. (*Bastard son of cocksucking motherfuck! Yes! You, my friend!*)

"What was his name?" Gabriel asked.

"Who?" Simon said.

"The nudist interpreter."

"Wesley. Wes. He picked his interpreter name because he loved Wesley Snipes movies–*Blade*, *Passenger 57*, even *Demolition Man*. Dude wouldn't shut up about *New Jack City*." Simon smiled, looked down at the empty coffee cup in his hands. Then he met my eyes. "Wes. All gas, no brakes, that guy."

I heard things that Ettie, Claire, and Gabriel didn't. Things both Simon and I were glad the other understood, but that we wouldn't say aloud. As if we had an unspoken pact not to sully the language of peace with descriptions of war.

Claire cleared the coffee cups from the living room table after the boys left.

From the couch, Ettie and I listened to Claire fussing in the kitchen. Ettie stood up. "I should help."

"Yeah, me too." Creaking like an old man, I rose from the couch.

"He smiles more," Ettie said.

I nodded, walked to the window, and parted the drapes just in time to see the taillights of Simon's truck disappearing from our cul-de-sac.

You made it, son. Now comes the hard part.

Dewaine Farria is a former enlisted U.S. Marine and U.N. field security officer. As a Marine, he served in Jordan and Ukraine. As an employee of the United Nations, he served in Kenya, Somalia, Occupied Palestine, and the North Caucasus. He works for the Asian Development Bank, and lives in the Philippines with his wife and children. Vietnam War veteran and author Tobias Wolff selected Farria's first novel, Revolutions of All Colors, *as the winner of Syracuse University Press' first Veterans Writing Contest. Farria's work appears widely in print and on-line. He holds a Master of Fine Arts in Creative Writing from Vermont College of Fine Arts, and a graduate degree in international studies from the University of Oklahoma.*

Village with No Name

By Ray McPadden
Third-Place Prose, 2017

The RPG cage rattled as the Stryker barreled down the doubletrack road. The patrol leader, Sgt. 1st Class Burns, stood in the commander's hatch with tight fists and his checkered scarf up to his eyes. Burns told himself to be cool. Inside, he was flapping like a hooked trout. Tonight, their target was a safehouse for a Sunni militia captain. This was a mission no one wanted, for there was a sandstorm brewing in the eastern desert. If caught in the blinding sand, Burns' men would be cutoff from air cover and medevac. The platoon would beat the storm if shit didn't go sideways. Be cool, Burns told himself again.

They snaked through the stinking streets of Al-Hayy. As they navigated the roundabouts, Burns issued commands to the driver. "In at the six, out at the twelve." Then, "In at the six, out at the three." Checking over his shoulder, Burns saw the four Strykers in tail holding their intervals. On they went. Burns was calm, at least on the outside

A half-hour into the drive, they crossed a median south of Al-Hayy. Exposed rebar in the median flattened two tires on the second Stryker. They halted for a tire change. Burns said, "Shit has gone sideways."

The radio beeped, "2-7, this is 2-2. Blue Force Tracker shows an engineer convoy two klicks west. They've probably got a power-jack. Let's get 'em on the horn."

Burns answered, "I ain't asking pot-bellied engineers for help." As a matter of principle, Burns didn't ask others for help. It was poor form in the infantry.

A red-faced corporal from 1st Squad fumbled with the hydraulic jack in the dark. Burns snatched the jack and set it himself. He then threw in a twist of tobacco and wrenched off the lug nuts. The corporal was standing there looking dumb, so Burns told him, "Grab Alpha Team and get me two fuckin' tires, like yesterday," and the corporal was running before Burns finished the sentence. Four sweaty men set the new tires and the platoon was moving again, a half-hour behind schedule.

Once more, Burns stood tall in the TC hatch, his body exposed above the waist, as if he'd already forgotten about the two IEDs the night before. The Strykers topped out at 55 mph, their pistons pumping inside turbocharged engines. The sweet scent of diesel combustion vanished in the wind. There was only the clean smell of the desert. Burns loved that smell.

The squad in back of Burns' Stryker were all standing half out the hatches, sweeping their guns and lasers across the palms and blackrock desert. Sgt. Garcia stood closest to the ramp, silenced MP5 pulled into his shoulder. He was slaying dogs for no particular reason. "Did you see that shot?" said Garcia, lasering the dog he had just dropped, "On the move at 50 meters. It's hard being this good."

The badlands in the east were sun-cracked. Sand dunes marked the horizon where the storm would come from. About 0345, the platoon pulled up short of an unnamed village and scanned with thermals. Burns spied what looked to be a colony of sand castles ringed by a palm grove. Inside the village, lampposts and courtyard floods cast hoops of dim light, but no one stirred.

Burns told the driver, "Shoot the gap, there–don't slow down," and they were off again. Reaching the village, they rumbled through the main thoroughfare without tapping the brakes. Burns saw electric lines ahead. The twisting network of lines were strung up between the houses, running up and down and crisscrossing the road. Some ran lengthwise to a rookery of huts that must have been the village bazaar. This tangled web was the power grid, the arteries and veins of a clay village that seemed a biological extension of the desert.

The squad boys in the back hatches ducked to avoid being clotheslined. Burns' Stryker turret ripped down the first few lines, which twisted and knotted over the hull. There were flashes and sparks and cracks of electricity as more lines snapped off and whipped about. On they went, bringing down more lines. What the turret missed, the Stryker's antennae did not, and by the far end of the village, a few dozen electric lines were wrapped around Burns' Stryker, some dragging behind it, some still glowing with current. Burns rose in the hatch, saying, "Everyone up," through the intercom. The squad boys in back emerged like gophers and aimed once more at the desert. Behind them, the village was now dark. The platoon crossed into palm groves, and three miles on, they halted at the rally point.

They circled the Strykers, dismounted, and hustled into a screen of grasses and reeds. A half mile later, they blew in the target house's metal door with a water charge. A man with bed-head and a Kalashnikov came running down the stairs to see about the fuss. Burns shot him in the face and his head exploded like a water balloon across a tiled wall where a family picture hung. Burns kicked away the gun and stepped over the body. The assault squads fanned through the rooms. They cleared the house in one long minute, but their man was nowhere to be found. They tossed the rooms. Garcia smashed dinner plates on the kitchen floor where two old women sat wailing. They left the women on the floor and exited the house.

Burns marched for the Strykers as dawn reared up brown in the east. In came the first grains of the storm. Burns blinked sand from his eyes, and radioed Garcia, "Storm's a' coming." First Squad emerged from the house carrying plastic bags with confiscated cell phones and thumb drives and digital paraphernalia. They trotted for the Strykers, once more crossing the palm grove, following the same swath they had trampled during their silent infil. Burns waved at them to hurry.

Garcia skittered through the grass and came up panting, telling Burns, "Thought you might try to leave us." Just then, Garcia yelped and jumped and ran wildly ahead. He only made it 20 feet before he dropped. Garcia rolled, calling out, "Something bit me! Something bit me!" There was panic in his voice. It all happened in a blink.

Turning on his rifle-mounted flashlight, Burns scanned the grass. There he saw a cobra with shiny skin and vertical pupils. When it hissed, the venom on its fangs glistened in the flashlight beam. The cobra had the girth of a man's forearm. Its tail rested somewhere unseen in the chest-high grass. Taking a bead, Burns fired twice. The second bullet split the head, which slumped onto the twitching body. Burns ran back to Garcia, and found the squad boys huddled around him. Elbowing through the crowd, Burns saw that Garcia' leg was swelling badly, the skin cherry-colored. Doc kneeled over Garcia and produced a set of surgical scissors and cut off Garcia's boot.

Doc looked up at Burns, "This is bad. What bit him?"

Burns said, "A cobra. Where's the anti-venom?"

With edge in his voice, Doc said, "Fucking anti-venom? Sarge, what you think this is?"

"You don't have any?"

Garcia broke in with groans and then a mortal scream. He thrashed and pedaled in a circle, flattening a little landing in the grass.

Doc held him still and told Burns, "Anti-venom?! I fix holes. I ain't no snake doctor."

Burns said, "We've got no air support. It's an hour and twenty back to the COP. How long's he got?"

"A cobra bite? Shit, uh." Doc rose and whispered to Burns, "He'll be dead by the time we get back. We need a bird."

Burns said, "They'll never fly in this storm."

"Maybe we ask the village north of here."

"The one we just came through?"

Doc shrugged his shoulders. "Or we could go back to the target. I'm sure those old hags in the kitchen would be happy to help."

"Goddammit," said Burns. He dreaded the idea of asking for help, especially since the platoon had just destroyed the village grid.

Doc said, "What choice do we have?"

Burns scratched his chin for a bit, and said, "Mount up."

They pulled up in the village at 0700. The first squall of sand was ripping through the houses. Bits of trash skipped through the alleys. The palms dotting the dirt streets shook violently against the storm's power. They had only a few minutes before the storm descended fully upon them.

At this point, thought Burns, a bird was out of the question and it would be a long, slow drive back to the outpost. The options were cruel. Up ahead, a group of bearded old men were marching down the street, coming right for the Strykers. Pulling his scarf up against the stinging grains, Burns jumped from the hatch and strode toward the men. Burns guessed they were the village elders. One leather-faced old man stomped forward and met Burns. In his right hand the old man held a coil of black wire.

The old man held up the wire. There was anger in his tired eyes. "You did this."

Burns opened his mouth to lie about it. He realized the same black lines were still draped across his Stryker. "We didn't see them in the dark."

"You rip down the lines and we put them back up and you rip them down again," said the old man. "This is not good for my boy. He needs a machine to breathe. He suffers when you kill the power."

Burns said, "I'm sorry for your son." Burns squirmed in his body armor. He didn't want to say what he was about to. "We need your help."

"Help?"

"Yes. A cobra bit one of our men."

"Why should I help men who take away our power?"

"We are new here. The soldiers you speak of are gone, back to the States." Burns was telling the truth. "Now we are here and things will be different." Burns wasn't sure that part was true.

The old man looked at the wall of sand in the east.

Burns tugged his shoulder. "Chief, can you help us?"

The old man said, "You, the Ameriki, ask the help of my tribe."

"Our man doesn't have much time."

"What of your helicopters?" asked the old man, "What of your planes?"

"The storm keeps them on the ground."

The old man smirked. "You ask me." He didn't seem to believe what he was hearing. "We'll help on one condition. Promise me this – from now on, you'll go around our village. You'll not spoil our electric scheme."

Burns put his hand over his heart. "I swear, Chief, as long as I'm here, no one will interfere with your electric lines."

Leather-face went back to the elders and they exchanged clipped words. They began shouting at each other and the chief and the Americans. At last, the elders summoned a boy on a rooftop, who ran down the street and disappeared.

Minutes later, the boy returned holding an old woman by the elbow. The old woman wore a black cloak over her curved back. She carried a jar filled with jade-colored paste. Alpha team searched her and then dropped the ramp on the Stryker, revealing Garcia lying on a stretcher in the cabin. Garcia's leg was turning green. His face was ghostly white and glazed with sweat. The woman hobbled up the Stryker ramp with her cloak wheeling in the wind. She sat on her heels and went to work with her paste.

Watching all this, Burns stood beside the old man and the boy.

The old man rubbed his white beard and told Burns, "The boy who brought this woman, once, he was bitten when out with the goats. We used the paste on him. It attacks the venom."

The young boy must have heard the tale being recalled, for he hiked up one leg of his track pants. There was a brown scar at midcalf. It looked as if the skin there had been removed with an ice cream scoop. The boy fingered the scar and then held his chin high, looking very proud of himself.

Burns told the boy, "You're a brave boy. Braver than me." Then Burns put a hand over his own heart again and addressed the old man. "Thanks, Chief. I'm grateful, and know this – I keep my word."

The old man said, "You must get your man to a doctor quickly or he'll lose the leg. He will be well, *Inshallah*."

"As soon as she's done," said Burns, "We'll move on."

"Remember our village, remember our electric scheme." Pointing east, the old man said, "There is a track through the grove, it's good driving, clear and wide. If you come back again, use it to go around. We'll mend the potholes just for you."

"If we hear of bad men in the village," said Burns, "We must come in."

"So be it," said the old man, "But you'll find no evil men here. Maybe on the farms, but not in the village. Nothing escapes my eye."

"I promise we'll go around," said Burns, "You're a good man, Chief. You're on our team. We take care of our team. Rebuild your power lines. No more harm will come to them. You're under our care now."

The old man said, "Thank you." He closed his eyes for a moment against the sand, which now came in slants. "It's my boy I think of."

About that time, the old woman finished with Garcia and capped her jar and disappeared in the blowing sand. The platoon mounted again and set off with Garcia moaning over his leg. Burns waved goodbye to the chief. They rounded a bend and rolled on into blowing sand.

A week later, Burns swung open the door of the plywood hut they called HQ. He picked up the red phone and listened to the report on Garcia. The old woman's paste had done well. The main ingredient came from a plant called *paniculata*, long used by the natives as an anti-venom. Garcia would keep his leg. He'd be back after two weeks of R&R.

That afternoon, some boys from JSOC rolled into their outpost in armored jeeps. Burns had his feet up on the desk in HQ, listening to the battalion radio update when a long-haired Operator came into HQ. A tiger-striped rifle was slung across his chest. He moseyed up to Burns, saying his name was Nick. Nick wanted to know about routes to the north. He unfolded a map on the desk in front of Burns. Nick said they had just crossed through the southern part of Burns' battlespace.

"Down south," said Nick, "There was this little village that had no name on the map." Nick pointed to the village on the map.

Burns gulped when he saw it was the chief's village.

Nick went on, "About 0800, we drove through. We must of clipped 200 powerlines. Half are still hanging off my jeep. This leather-faced old man was throwing rocks at us. One broke my windshield. No shit, that old man threw a rock through a bulletproof windshield." Nick laughed so hard his shoulders trembled. "That old bastard was pissed. I wouldn't go down there for a while." Nick was still laughing about it when he left.

Burns puffed his cheeks as he blew out a long, frustrated breath. He picked up the red phone for Battalion. When the supply officer announced himself on the line, Burns asked if anyone had any goddamn powerline poles.

Ray McPadden served as an infantry officer with the U.S. Army's 10th Mountain Division and Second Ranger Battalion, leading elite troops on four combat tours in Iraq and Afghanistan. He was awarded the Purple Heart, two Bronze Stars, and a medal for valor. His debut novel, And the Whole Mountain Burned, *was the 2019 Winner of the American Library Association's W.Y. Boyd Literary Award. His memoir,* We March at Midnight, *is forthcoming from Blackstone Publishing. McPadden now lives in Montana with his family.*

Air Born

By Eric Chandler
First-Place Poetry, 2017

a portajohn in Kyrgyzstan
one of my favorite pieces of graffiti:
Toodles, Afghanistan

our chartered airplane followed the great circle west
over territory I didn't recognize
a long sweep of coastline
probably The Maritimes
the sun gleamed down
through the severe clear

over the St. Croix
between Maine and Canada
reversing waterfalls are nearby
one direction when the tide flows
and the other when it ebbs
I knew where I was then

over the White Mountains
tiny from the air and
vast in my memory
my Limmer boots walked over
forty-eight peaks
I saw my birthplace

I tapped my friend on the shoulder
in the seat in front of me
I pointed down
with a war hangover and said
I was born there
Littleton

we slid across the northern tier

over the Upper Peninsula

over the old runways
he pointed down
I was born there
Kincheloe

faces plastered to the window over the
places we appeared by accident

Eric "Shmo" Chandler is a husband, father, and pilot who cross-country skis as fast as he can in Northern Minnesota. His poetry collection Hugging This Rock: Poems of Earth & Sky, Love & War *was published in 2017. He is also the author of a collection of outdoor essays called* Outside Duluth, *and a novella titled* Down In It. *His writing has appeared in* Northern Wilds, Grey Sparrow Journal, The Talking Stick, Flying Magazine, Sleet Magazine, O-Dark-Thirty, *and* Aqueous, *as well as others. He is a member of Lake Superior Writers, the Outdoor Writers Association of America, and the Military Writers Guild. Chandler is also a veteran of both the U.S. Air Force and the Minnesota Air National Guard. He flew 145 combat missions and more than 3,000 hours in the F-16. He served in Iraq and Afghanistan. He enjoys cross-country ski racing and marathon running. He lives with his wife and two children in Duluth, Minnesota.*

Facing 2003

By Jeremy Hussein Warneke
Second-Place Poetry, 2017

In a black notebook, hardcover
and college-ruled, Adam
Wobegon, an admirer of Yusef
Komunyakaa, writes the following
in black permanent ink:

My white hand fades,
deep inside the pale blue bucket.
I said I wouldn't
dammit: No washing.
I'm water. I'm flesh.
My clouded reflection eyes me
like a bird of prey ...
... I turn
this way–the water lets me go.
I turn that way–I'm inside
the wash bucket basin
again, depending upon the soap
to make a difference.
I go down the piles of clothes,
half-expecting to find
my old uniform encrusted in dirt.
I touch what looks like brown Army briefs;
I see the pink bucket's splash.
Clothes shimmer on the line outside ...
It's meant as a joke, but
there it is, staring starkly back
at him. The problem,
the dilemma. Always the same.
To wash, or not to wash:
Out of a bucket?
Adam swore that once he left Iraq–
more than ten years ago–

he would say *bon voyage*
forever to the tiresome task.
Now divorced and on the verge of
being dumped by
his newly pregnant girlfriend,
Adam concludes the poem–
among other things–by writing:
Once you go Iraq, you don't
go back.

*Jeremy Hussein Warneke is a public servant in the Bronx, New York. He
enlisted in the U.S. Army National Guard prior to 9/11 and subsequently
served in Iraq. His work has been appeared in* Scintilla; Task & Purpose;
the anthology Why We Write: Craft Essays on Writing War; *and
elsewhere. In 2016, with Voices From War and support from the Bronx
Council on the Arts, the New York Public Library, and his warneke
family, Jeremy launched "The Craft of War Writing" workshop, which
provides free, high-level reading and writing instruction for veterans and
the public, based upon the themes of conflict and war.*

The Frequency Hop

By Randy Brown
Third-Place Poetry, 2017

During World War II, Hollywood bombshell Hedy Lamarr
invented a method of encrypting communications
between a submarine and a torpedo on its way to target.

Two radios could hop around the spectrum, working in harmony, a
handshake tuned by hardware more at home with punch cards and
player pianos.

Every time I push-to-talk and hear
the synchronous COMSEC beep,
I think of that cartoonist's quote about Ginger Rogers:

"She did everything Fred Astaire did,
except backwards and in high heels."

*Randy Brown embedded with his former Iowa Army National Guard unit
as a civilian journalist in Afghanistan, May-June 2011. A 20-year veteran
with one overseas deployment, he subsequently authored the 2015 poetry
collection* Welcome to FOB Haiku: War Poems from Inside the Wire.
*His poetry and non-fiction have appeared widely in literary print and on-
line publications. A member of the Military Writers Guild, he co-edited
along with Steve Leonard the 2019 anthology* Why We Write: Craft
Essays in Writing War. *He often blogs as "Charlie Sherpa."*

2018

Some Kind of Storm

By Travis Klempan
First-Place Prose, 2018

John Mackenzie's eyes snapped open. He stared into the fuzzy purpling sky and decided not to move until he figured out what the hell had happened.

Met four hippies at Dallas-Fort Worth and agreed to tag along on their poorly detailed road trip. Gone one hundred miles in a custom camper van before he even thought to ask where they were going. The closest man–Tom? Thom?–handed Mack a flyer, calligraphied names listed alongside images of birds and cowboys. They'd crossed the Texas state line as he read *Abel Body ... Bloodspeak ... 10Penny Nails ... Crows w/White Bodies ... Three-Minute Hurricanes ...*

Mack looked up.

"These sound like death-metal bands," he'd shouted over the grumble of the overtaxed engine.

Thom laughed. "We prefer the term '*life*-metal'!" He looked like a blond Adam Sandler.

Tent City miles from anywhere, middle of nowhere, Oklahoma. Stages and microphones, amplifiers and Ferris wheels, Porta Johns and cotton candy machines, an entire carnival in the least hospitable place in America. Not as hot as Iraq, but dustier.

"The rancher lets us use his land for free. He was a big time California dope grower in the Sixties," Thom said. "He found Jesus and now he's the friendliest guy in Oklahoma." Mack followed the four men through the gates and into the bedlam.

He lost track of the hippies in less than an hour. Hundreds of bodies, sharing the sun and the sweat as Christian rock and Christian heavy metal and Christian rap rang out from competing speakers, mixing and muddling in the air and in his ears and in his stomach.

Beautiful and ugly humans, bodies of shapes and sizes he hadn't seen in months. What kind of history or explanation could he offer these people who had no clue where he'd been three days prior or would be three weeks hence, people he hadn't known existed until this moment? What kind of world was this?

Mack ate and listened to music and drank what was handed to him and nodded along politely as people talked of orthodoxy and heterodoxy, which bands were fortifying spirits and which weren't up to the task, who was touring where and what states had been skipped over on the festival's ramble across North America. He watched the bands sweat into the microphones, drowning themselves out with their appeals for love and each other and can't a man just love his fellow man without a lot of judgment *amen*?

As the sun set low against endless hills Mack wandered in front of a stage decorated with images of seagulls and cardinals. He split his attention between the band called *HandShake* and the people who clearly loved the band called *HandShake*, who had perhaps traveled for days to see the band called *HandShake*. There were dozens, maybe less than a hundred, but they were so intense and intent a crowd of meat pressed tight together and expanding with the set, thumping bass and meticulous guitar contracting and inflating the mass of human beings in rhythmic synchronization. He felt the epicenter of a giant lung, or a fish newly returned to the sea, sucking down oxygen for life.

And there, standing in front of him, Mack saw the Painted Man for the first time. A giant near 7 feet tall, bare-skinned to the waist, brute musculature shadowed and inked under the line of a thousand needles and flood lights swarming with moths. His clean-shaven head sported a wreath of thorns, railroad tracks crisscrossing his skull, and an all-seeing eye keeping watch behind him. His neck told the story of David and Goliath, his back the epic of Noah and his Ark, tales of tiger stripes and jungled canopies dripping down his flanks. Mack looked closer and he could see half the Zodiac encircling the man's shoulders.

His torso angled into a trim waist and the tattoos followed–lizards and scorpions picking apart images of skeletal waste seeping through his flesh. Mack moved through the crowd so he could see the backs of the man's calves and they were as tree trunks, plunging into root structures and secrets beneath the earth and his ankles.

He wanted to spin the man around, though the metaphor towered over the rest of the crowd. Mackenzie wanted to knock him down and examine his body, rip off his clothing and see how deep and far the tattoos extended. Was he drawn on the inside? Were his palms tapestries, his groin illuminated with the story of Adam and Eve?

Mack was tired, and drunk, and high, and had no clue how many miles it was to Baghdad or Dillinger or home if he had one or anywhere but here. He knew here was Oklahoma but only because the fifth hippie—had there been five? Four? Any?—said so and the "Welcome to Oklahoma" sign confirmed. The red earth tasted of iron and sun and he knew he was sick. Sun sick even as it set behind burnt hills.

Mackenzie stumbled out of the crowd and found refuge in the lee of a tent. The 2-degree difference in the weak haze felt like a new world to him. Someone offered him water and he took what he could, throwing most of it up. He had vague memories of bodies lifting him, an IV, a needle in his arm and a cool compress against his forehead. He smiled himself stupid under the gaze of volunteer medics. To survive Diyala Province and Operation Blacksmith and the donkey whisperer and the Mickey Mouse IED and two tours before and how many to come and to die of heat stroke in Oklahoma—who would tell *that* story? Someone should, he laughed.

The next morning he felt better. His head clear, fluids replenished, he could now walk under his own power. Mack politely shrugged off the offers of evacuation to the nearest town—two hours away over torn county roads and not much of a town on the other end—and promised to drink more water and nothing else, eat something bland if he could hold it down, un-fried if he could find it. He stumbled away from the medical tent, at once grateful and embarrassed that they'd refused payment.

Mack resumed his search for the Painted Man. With his head on straight he could talk to the man, ask for the meaning behind the tattoos, and see their full extent. He wouldn't need to dissect the Painted Man to unravel his mysteries and interpret the stories and sing them out loud in the voice of his people and *shit* was he still sick again?

Mackenzie saw the Painted Man loom large as a pillar. Whether he was ill or not he would confront him this time, and if he collapsed at the tattooed soles—bird's claws? Feet of a shark?—he would at least have come closer to learning… *I had to break to save the pain* …

Mack stopped short when the Painted Man turned. A series of images burned into the soldier's memory—the summer half of the Zodiac encircling the Man's collarbones—an epic battle between frigates unfolding across the Man's chest—his stomach displaying Joshua and the trumpet blasts at Jericho—his sides giving life to leopards and birds, leaping across his ribs in vivid patterns of light and dark.

His face.

Cheeks streaked with black tears, forehead bore witness to chapter and verse, nose covered in skeletal relief ... *This back weren't made for breaking* ... and then the Painted Man stepped aside, never seeing the soldier who hunted him, and John saw a woman.

The woman.

Later he would know her as Sera Quarron. Before he knew her name all he wanted was to hear her reveal it to him and that would have been enough in this life.

She stood alone, half-turned away from Mack, and he wanted to know her. He wanted her to let him know her. Black hair, the color of the distance between galaxies, straight and short and blowing, slender limbs and strong and full of life. Her shoulders visible beneath a white tank top, heralding the dawn through the boughs of a sycamore, branches reaching to her arms, in full leaf, a mighty tree brushed across the back of this woman. The trunk extended down, towards her waist, and he wondered at the roots.

Wings covered her arms—the feathered wing of an angel on her left, the leathered wing of a bat on her right. Symbols descended past her elbows, cryptic logos and characters spilling stories of mystery.

She turned and John saw her face and she looked at him and they stopped, or at least he hoped she stopped and looked at him. She smiled and he hoped forever that in the moment he smiled back. She was beautiful, and strong, and her eyes looked right into his and not to the side or above or beyond. She saw him and he saw her.

She was the first person in months to see him without looking past.

He walked forward, hoping she wouldn't dissolve into fugged air or slip into his subconscious.

The music changed. He had no idea who played—*Crows W/White Bodies? Bloodspeak?*—and the thrumming of the guitars replaced by the expansive keening of a cello, he thought it was a cello, had to be a cello, anything but a cello would be insufficient to the moment and he knew it. He didn't look at the stage but at her.

She turned her back on him in an invitation, stepped back towards him, and she crossed her arms. The white tank top, stark against her body ... *Tomorrow's already a promise broken* ... he could see the red straps of her bra and she was warm under the power of the sun and wind and soft under his fingers as they brushed years off her shoulders. She turned her head, looked up at him, and he pulled back.

Her eyes were not warnings but questions, curiosity meeting hesitation. He paused and let his arms fall to the side. She turned back and they both moved in time to the music and each other.

Her arms and chest showed birds and vegetation, an entire forest of life bounding across her body. Her bare legs held entire oceans of sea creatures, and his head swam.

Somehow they spoke—Sera with an *e*, she explained, Quarron with a *q*. She answered his questions quickly, easily, asking her own and waiting for his answers, leaning close to listen and speak over the music. She must have pegged him as a soldier instantly, but gave no voice to those thoughts. He sensed an immediate wall and her conscious tearing down of that wall, and the last thing she told him as the last song started was "Find me again." The crowd rose like the birth of an ocean and they parted.

He scanned the human current for her black hair or white shirt, the blood flash of lipstick or bra, searching stupidly for the peculiar cross she wore on a leather strap tight around her neck ... *Don't let me go ...*

Find me again, she'd said. Words echoed over the thrum of music and humanity.

Find me.

Again.

Hours later—he searched, his head and stomach clearing after the sickness of that morning, his heart beating against his chest slow but burdened—Mack saw giant black clouds piling up on the horizon. A storm of any size would soak the dusty fields, make rivers of mud erupt and weave out of dance floors and carnival midways. The weakest breeze would surely topple the speakers and the scaffolding, one bolt of lightning would toss the Ferris wheel down, and this was no storm of just any size.

The hurricane came, as foreseen and foretold and worse. Mackenzie sought shelter with other human refugees under a giant canopy until it ripped, laden with rainwater and slashed by hail. They scattered and he wandered across the belly of his nation, red mud painting his body as the sun died forever behind menacing clouds. He remembered Tent City to the west, higher ground at the campsite, so he followed what remained of his internal compass and collapsed at the same time as the storm came again, howling wind giving a last shrieking challenge to the land.

He dreamed of being buried under centuries of mud, entombed in the barrows of the planet, all the animals from the Painted Man's Ark laughing at him.

And then—as now—he was awake and fully remembered where and what he was. He was on the ground, on his back, staring into the warming blue of an eggshell sky. He assumed he was still in Oklahoma but would not have been surprised to find himself back in Mesopotamia, or Oz, or Hell.

A rock jabbed Mackenzie in the small of his back. He decided to let it, for now, as he finished assembling his memories and considered the day. If he tilted his head back he saw hints of red and orange. If it were morning that meant his feet pointed west; if evening then east. The dome above was wet and crystalline, soft as a blanket but completely unbroken by clouds. Probably morning, though he couldn't pick why.

A small brown cross circled high above. Bird, he thought. Vulture? His lips curled—was it here to eat him? Had he died? He tried to hear the scavenger, listen to its gut and learn its story, especially if it was the last thing he'd hear.

Not a vulture, he realized. A hawk of common breed. Not hunger but curiosity, even caution, especially this early. Maybe he weren't dead yet.

Mack's hand slid beneath his body and clutched the rock when he heard the growl. A low and primal warning bloomed from the direction of his feet, freezing him in place. *West*, some small part of his brain reminded him. His arm wedged beneath him, Mackenzie lifted his head and focused on a coyote no farther than a few feet from his naked toes. He'd never been this close to a wild animal, so the fear took a moment to register.

"What're you supposed to be," he said, voice cracking dry, "my spirit animal?"

The creature was lean, powerful, nothing wasted on its spare frame. The coyote didn't speak. The eyes were smart and keen, looking right at—

Not looking at him. She was looking at a spot on the ground between his feet.

He lowered his eyes to the same spot.

He saw the viper.

He heard the rattle.

John flinched. The snake struck, mouth open and fangs extended, aiming for his bare foot. The coyote was faster, grabbing the snake just behind its head and thrashing it to death in a second. The rattler hung limp from the coyote's jaws. She turned from Mackenzie, trotted away, and stopped. She swung her feral head back and he swore the coyote winked at him.

The animal departed–loping easily and efficiently across the muddy plains, away from the campsite and towards the wild brush to enjoy her breakfast–and he heard laughter behind him. He spun, as surprised as when the snake attacked, and saw Sera.

She sat with her legs folded underneath her, denim shorts and black bra and no other threads on her body, the small wooden cross topped with a circle resting in the notch between her collarbones, burning cigarette dangling from slender fingers. She stopped laughing and smiled.

"More like a guardian angel, I'd wager." She sucked on the cigarette and exhaled a spiral of bluish grey. "That was pretty fucking holy."

He smiled, repositioning himself to face her. "How long you been watching?" She passed him a cigarette and offered her lighter. Her body was as clean as his was muddy.

"If I say Long Enough it's gonna sound cliché," she said, scratching behind her ear. "But long enough."

"Did you see the snake?" He glanced west. She shook her head. "The coyote?" She nodded. "How did we–"

"I told you to find me." She shrugged. "So I guess you did."

John looked around as he lit up. Her tent lay in a pile behind her, battered by the storm, and tents and sleeping bags and camper trailers close aboard showed signs of the prairie hurricane. "Some storm last night," he said.

She laughed, sprinkling glass and bell music. "That was no mere storm. Never been a storm like that, not here, likely won't be again. That was a chapter closing, John Mackenzie, a book opening up, the heavens sending us a signal to rejoice and be fearful and wake the fuck up." She smiled brightly. "But yeah, hell of a storm."

She spoke without accent, at least none he could detect. The sun had burned her shoulders, forearms, the parts of her chest not covered by cloth. She was once again beautiful but he had no clue what to say next.

She spoke first. "You heading there? Coming back?" She exhaled another plume. "Or something else?"

He propped himself up more comfortably. "In between. I've got to head back in … twelve days?" He counted in his head. "Eleven."

"You a big fan of contemporary religious music, John Mackenzie? Getting your fix of spirituality before you go back?"

He shook his head and laughed. "Not really. You?"

"I'm a fan of life, and only a temporary believer of any sort." She stubbed the cigarette out in the dirt beneath her legs and lit another one. "Why limit ourselves?"

John looked at Sera and an image of her body curled against his flashed into his mind. He didn't know if it was memory or fantasy. He took a gamble. "Did we …"

She laughed and shook her head, her black bangs hanging over her eyebrows and her short ponytail swinging freely. "No, we did not. You found my tent near midnight, mumbled something about donkeys and stomach flu, and collapsed. Slept a few hours inside, then insisted on counting stars after the second storm passed." She squinted at him. "I think you been sick, John." She held the smoke in her lungs for a long heartbeat. "Can I say something, hope you don't take offense?" She smirked. "Sorry, guess I answered my own question. You cry out in your sleep. Who're Cisneros and Ledbetter?"

Mackenzie felt his heart blast, one insane surge against his chest wall, and he felt like he might throw up. "I gotta go." He stood, dizzy and weak, and Sera stood with him.

"You don't want to talk about them or anything else you don't have to." She was short, atomic in the presence of his body, but stood her ground fierce. "You never want to speak their story, that's OK, too."

She didn't ask him to stay or come. She didn't offer excuses. She didn't say anything beyond her apology but the way she stood in front of him left no choice but to lower his defenses. He relaxed his fists, which he hadn't realized were clenched. His shoulders slumped. She was a molecule but big as a mountain. He might not be recovered from the flu or the storm or the coyote or the war but he sensed something in her stance that prevented him from leaving, made him want to stay.

"What are you?" he asked for the first time again, smiling.

She smiled back. "You said you had 11 days?" He nodded. "Where you going?"

Travis Klempan was born and raised in Colorado. He joined the U.S. Navy to see the world. After realizing most of it is water, he returned to the Mile High state, collecting degrees in English, creative writing, and ethics along the way. He is the author of the 2020 novel Have Birds, Need Snakes, *from which this story is excerpted. His short fiction and poetry have appeared in such literary venues as* Proximity, Windmill, *and* Bombay Gin. *He helped launch a short-lived guerrilla zine, and his short story "Two Fingers Down" was nominated by the Veterans Writing Project for a 2017 Pushcart prize. He lives in Colorado with his wife, two cats, and two dogs.*

Green

By Brian L. Braden
Second-Place Prose, 2018

This is the edge of the world, where all light ends, she thought.

There are many shades of darkness, and now she faced the deepest, blackest shade of all. Not a single flicker of light penetrated the abyss– not a car, a house, not even a campfire. Starved for light, the ghostly green image in her night vision goggles sparkled and flickered.

The copilot still wasn't comfortable wearing the aviator's night-vision goggles. Suspended from her helmet, they looked like two toilet paper rolls duct taped together. They transformed the blackness beyond their lenses into a fuzzy fluorescent green universe, denying night her ancient cloak of secrecy.

At over a hundred-and-thirty miles per hour, the helicopter skated over calm, frozen air. She felt as if floating motionless in a green Ping-Pong ball. The lack of vibration and apparent motion denied her brain the sensations it craved.

Through the goggles, only a blurry line separating two different shades of dark green betrayed the faint horizon. It, and an occasional glance at the softly-glowing instruments, provided her only clues to the universe beyond the cockpit. With this trickle of sensory input a 120-pound woman kept the 10-ton helicopter right-side-up and pointed toward its destiny. The copilot's universe consisted of the image the goggles fed her hungry eyes, the cockpit gauges' soft glow, and voices filling her head.

She shared the helicopter strapped to her back with three other crewmen. Before the mission they had real names, but were now only known by their roles: pilot, right gunner, and left gunner. They had 'compartmentalized,' existing only for this moment, this mission.

The Team sat on the cold metal floor against the aft bulkhead, knees pulled up against their chest in casual misery. Not a part of the crew, these men were tonight's customers and cargo. Cradling their weapons, they kept their night-vision goggles flipped up. This part of the mission did not belong to them. Powerless to affect its outcome, they preferred not to watch, satisfied in the dark, each alone with his thoughts until their moment for action arrived.

"Altitude and airspeed are good. Heading is good," the pilot announced over the intercom as he spat chewing tobacco into a styrofoam cup. The faint, tobacco sweet odor permeated the cockpit, but no one ever complained about his minor infraction of regulations.

The copilot relaxed her vise-like grip on the control stick, called a "cyclic," and flexed her right hand. With a deep breath, she lightly placed two fingers back on the cyclic.

"OK, crew, what's next?" the pilot said.

The moment upon which the rest of the mission depended rapidly approached.

"Gotta finish the checklist, sir," the right-gunner chimed in.

The copilot couldn't see the right- or left-gunner. They sat sideways, immediately behind each pilot, gripping heavy machine guns and scanning the darkness out each side. To the copilot, they were disembodied voices crackling in her helmet, blending with the helicopter's roar.

"All right, let's finish the checklist," the pilot said.

"Probe ... extend," the right gunner read mechanically from his checklist. Out of the corner of her eye she saw the right-gunner's arm, dimly reflected in the instrument lights, reach forward over the console for a switch.

A clunk reverberated under the floor, and the refueling probe slowly extended from the right side of the helicopter's nose. The tip jutted into the copilot's peripheral vision like a lance, until it halted with a thunk a meter beyond the whirling rotor disc.

"Extended and locked," the pilot replied as he adjusted a dial. In response, a feeble ray of light brightened the probe, revealing how uncomfortably close the rotor disk and probe tip were to each other. Beyond the probe, a shape caught the copilot's eye.

Mountain.

A gauntlet of snow-capped granite slowly materialized to either side. Her brain feasted on the visual references, providing a jolting awareness of how high and fast she flew. As if on cue, turbulent eddies of air rolled off the peaks and jostled the helicopter.

"A little chop, crew." Her voice cracked slightly, betraying rising anxiety. The turbulence, while expected, made her job even more demanding.

"Checklist completed," the right gunner said. "We're ready."

"Roger," the pilot replied. "I'm visual with the tanker. He's at our 10 o'clock, 2 miles, high, and closing."

The copilot glanced left in time to catch a dark blur zoom by in the opposite direction. Over a mile away, the giant tanker airplane appeared to scrape the canyon walls as it banked hard to swing in behind the helicopter.

"Tanker is 8 o'clock, three miles, and in a tight turn," the left gunner informed the crew. The copilot knew the gunner poked his head out the window by the sound of the wind roaring across his boom microphone.

OK, the pilot is going to take the controls anytime, she thought. There's no way he'll let me fly this.

The pilot remained silent.

"Tanker is at our six. Left-gunner's lost visual. Right-gunner, you should see him now." The roar momentarily stopped as the left-gunner withdrew his head into the helicopter, but quickly resumed as the right gunner stuck his head out the helicopter's opposite side.

"Got'em. He's at our five-thirty, 2 miles and closing fast," the right gunner called.

She tried to breathe, struggling not to tense up. The long years of training were over, and now real consequences lay before her. This mission would last several hours, but its success pivoted on this one moment.

The helicopter needed gas, and only this tanker could deliver it.

"Tanker is half-mile and bringing it in tight, almost on top of us." The roar over the intercom ceased as the right-gunner withdrew into the cabin and closed his window.

The pilot remained quiet, and off the controls.

He's actually going to let me fly the refueling, she thought in amazement.

"Tanker is abeam, damn tight. Start your climb now. Co, call visual," the right-gunner called.

Her moment had arrived. The copilot pulled up on the collective, the power lever in her left hand. Her right hand nudged the cyclic, and the helicopter obeyed with a sluggish climb.

She briefly scanned across the cockpit, expecting the tanker to emerge a few dozen meters outside the pilot's side window.

It didn't. In the faint light, she saw the pilot grin around the tobacco bulging in his cheek. He pointed up. She followed his finger.

In the overhead window, an enormous shadow swallowed the stars as it passed directly overhead. Deep bass concussions, sensed more than heard, pounded through the rotor blades.

"Shit, he's on top of us!" she blurted, but quickly regained her composure. "Copilot is visual with the tanker."

"*Goooood* tanker pilot," the pilot chuckled and spit in his cup again. "He did you a favor. Now you won't have to work so hard to get into position. OK, Co, get in there and get some gas."

The copilot guided her flying machine to a position just outside the airplane's left wing. A cargo plane converted to a flying gas station, the tanker's four giant propellers clawed the thin air, wallowing a razor's edge above stall speed. Five miles an hour slower, and it would spin out of control; any faster, and the helicopter couldn't keep up.

Through her goggles, she watched smooth jets of green flame dance from the tanker's exhaust nozzles, each brightening or dimming as the tanker pilot adjusted his throttles. Allowing herself a brief moment to admire the scene's beauty, she took another cleansing breath.

I can do this.

"Ground fire, 2 o'clock, 5 miles!" the left gunner barked.

She snapped her goggles left in time to see twinkling flashes arc into sky on the other side of the valley.

Training and instinct instantly kicked in, along with a burst of adrenaline. The copilot keyed the microphone to tell the tanker to break away due to the enemy fire. Before she could act, the pilot spoke up.

"It's not aimed," he spoke with slow, deliberate calmness before spitting again. "It's random fire. They can't see us, just shooting at echoes. If the tanker ain't worried, neither am I. Press on."

The tracers, and her adrenaline, burned out and vanished into the cold night.

A drogue parachute, about a meter across, popped out from a pod near the left wingtip. It blossomed in the slipstream, revealing a metal receptacle the size of a tea saucer at its center. The drogue slowly pulled a hose from the pod until it extended 30 meters behind the wing, where it danced a wicked figure-eight pattern abeam the tanker's tail.

Beyond the drogue, a lone sentinel stood on the tanker's open cargo ramp, only inches from the edge.

The loadmaster, this moment's gatekeeper, would signal the helicopter when they were cleared to refuel.

He must be freezing, she thought. Motionless behind his night vision goggles, the loadmaster betrayed nothing.

The cockpit heater switch remained off because it robbed the helicopter's engines of precious power. The cold soaked through the helicopter's thin skin, and into the copilot's fingers.

Darkness their only shield, the odd formation hung suspended above the valley floor. Built to fly high and fast, the tanker usually sought refuge among the clouds. The helicopter found safety hiding behind hills, and skimming over the trees. Like soldiers from another war, they found themselves in a "no man's land," exposed and vulnerable between trenches. Here, a few lucky bullets could doom them both. The safety of both aircraft depended on finishing the refueling quickly, so each could return to where it belonged.

The loadmaster flashed a light so dim she almost missed it.

"Green light," the right gunner said. "Cleared down and right. Understand pilot has the controls?" The last words burned in her ears.

"Negative," the pilot responded. "This is the copilot's plug."

"Uh ... *roger*," the right-gunner responded.

Determined, excited, resigned, terrified ... she tried to tamp down the conflicting emotions and focus on her first combat aerial refueling.

With the slightest pressure on the controls, she slid the helicopter right until it settled immediately behind the tanker's wing, and only a couple feet behind the drogue. From this perspective, the copilot could better see the turbulence jostling the tanker, its wingtips rocking up and down, whiplashing the refueling drogue. The rotor blades whirled only a few feet from the tanker's thin aluminum skin. Unconcerned, the sentinel on the cargo ramp continued his vigil.

"Pre-contact position," the copilot announced, trying to sound cool and confident.

Just like training, she reassured herself and tried concentrating on the tanker's wing as she'd been trained. Counter to what she knew she should do, her eyes followed the drogue's maddening dance and not the relatively stable wing. Her hands followed her eyes, and the helicopter shook and shimmied as she struggled to align the probe with the erratic target.

"Rising terrain, left side," the left gunner called as the valley floor slowly rose to meet them. In her goggles the ground came into focus, reminding her how little time remained. The peaks closed in with every mile. The helicopter couldn't climb higher, and soon the valley would be too narrow for the tanker to turn around.

She continued to chase the drogue. Lights across the instrument panel flashed yellow warnings, as the engines strained to deliver more power.

"Hey, Co, do you hear that whistling sound?" the pilot asked.

Over the screaming engines she barely detected the new sound.

"Yeah," she said tensely, the task threatening to overwhelm her.

"It's the wind whistling through the right gun. It means you're out of trim and over-controlling the aircraft."

She bit her lip at the realization she'd allowed the helicopter to cock slightly sideways, dragging the big tail rotor through the slipstream, costing precious power and airspeed.

"It's always best to keep your scan on the wing, just glance at the drogue every once in a while and relax. You're doing great." Without a hint of impatience or concern, he sounded more like a coach than a combat-seasoned aircraft commander.

She remembered to breathe and forced her eyes back on the tanker's wing. The tail resumed its proper place directly behind the helicopter, and the right gun ceased whistling. Some of the bumpiness went away, but not all.

"OK, good. Now, go for the plug."

"Roger, going for the plug." She nudged the helicopter forward and picked up speed. The probe inched toward the drogue, and, for a moment, appeared as if she would score a bulls-eye. The basket snapped to the right at the last second, and the probe missed by a few agonizing inches.

"A miss." She lowered the collective to avoid crashing into the wing only 10 meters ahead, and settled the helicopter behind the drogue again. "Going for another plug." She advanced toward the refueling drogue again, and missed.

Another miss, then another, and then another.

"Terrain is getting close on the left side, sir," the left-gunner reminded the pilot. The copilot knew what he really meant. *Please take the controls and get this shit over with.*

Frustrated, she dove at the drogue. Instead of the metal spokes leading to the inner receptacle, the probe caught the parachute material's edge. The drogue chute collapsed around the probe tip, and the metal spokes slammed against the tip in a shower of green sparks. A momentary puff of fuel sprayed the helicopter's right side. A brief whiff of kerosene mixed with the tobacco aroma, and she wondered if she'd damaged the probe.

She knew if the drogue didn't re-inflate, it would shred against the probe or, worse, entangle them. The tanker and helicopter would then be stuck together, unable to turn or climb out of the valley.

"Come straight back, nice and slow," the pilot warned.

She eased the helicopter backwards until the hose extended and flattened. With a slight jerk, the drogue released and re-inflated. Filled with relief, she let her concentration slip for only a moment.

The helicopter drifted insidiously to the right...toward the tanker.

"Stop right! *STOP RIGHT!*" The right-gunner screamed.

She felt the pilot snatch the controls and jam the cyclic left. Sucked in the twisting vortices generated by the plane's giant propellers, the helicopter shimmied violently and tried to roll into the tanker.

The sentinel on the cargo ramp took one step backwards.

"Pilot's controls," the pilot firmly commanded. "Pilot's controls." The copilot confirmed the pilot had the controls and released her hands.

She mentally kicked herself, realizing she'd blown an opportunity to prove herself.

Engines screamed and rotors slowed, as the pilot demanded every ounce of power to escape the tanker's monstrous wake turbulence. Only his skill and a few seconds stood between the helicopter smashing into the tanker, or flipping upside down and disintegrating. He dove down to the left and found clean air, but not before the helicopter fell far behind the tanker.

She could almost sense the right and left gunners covering their microphones and sighing in relief.

It costs precious minutes for the helicopter catch up. The sentinel on the cargo ramp once again sent the signal, clearing them to refuel.

The copilot caught a whiff of another smell mixing with the stink of the jet fuel and tobacco. Someone on the Team had vomited.

Crisply and smoothly, the pilot placed the helicopter immediately behind the drogue, ready to attempt another plug. The right and left gunners craned forward for a better view of the probe, now just inches away from the drogue. She knew they desperately wanted the master aviator to complete the connection and finish the job.

Part of her wanted him to finish the job, too.

"Copilot's controls," he directed.

Over the intercom, someone stifled a groan.

"Copilot's controls." Once more, she took the machine's reins.

"Listen," the pilot said, "You've got one more chance then I'm going to have to do this, understand?"

"Yes, sir." He knows what he's doing. He thinks I can do this, so I can do this.

"Just relax and remember your training." His tone soothed her nerves.

Despite the low light, snow, boulders, and other details on the mountains gelled into disturbing crispness in her goggles. She tried not to think about how close they looked, instead, focusing on the rocking wing and trying not to stare at the dancing drogue.

"OK crew, going for the plug." She pushed her machine forward once again.

Wing, wing, wing, drogue ... wing, wing, wing, drogue ... she repeated the mantra in her mind, ... wing, wing, wing, drogue ... wing, wing, wing, drogue ... wing, wing ...

Plunk!

Looking down, she saw the probe neatly lodged in the drogue's center.

"Good contact!" the right gunner exclaimed.

"Son-of-a-bitch! Cleared up and left!" the left gunner responded.

The copilot flew the helicopter up and away from the tanker, to a station just above and outside the wing tip. Like an umbilical cord, the hose fed the helicopter precious fuel. The right gunner ticked off the fuel status every few seconds, "20 percent ... 30 percent ... 50 percent ..."

Relief flooded over her. She only needed to hold this formation position for a few minutes and it would all be over.

The fuel tanks filled and the helicopter grew steadily heavier, requiring more power to keep aloft. To compensate, the copilot made subtle, unconscious control corrections.

Her corrections, however, weren't quite fast enough. She didn't notice the growing whistle, this time coming from the left gun.

"80 percent ... 90 percent ..." the right gunner continued the countdown.

"You're out of trim again. Give me a little left pedal," the pilot said.

She pressed her boot against the left pedal, but with too much pressure.

"Gently," he warned, but it was too late.

The nose jerked left. The snap, coupled with the damaged receptacle, caused the probe to disconnect without sealing.

POOF!

A cloud of jet fuel completely enveloped the helicopter. The windscreen transformed into a milky blur, blinding the crew to the world outside, including the tanker only meters away.

"Come straight back ... slowly ... slowly," the pilot coached. The copilot complied.

The right gunner must have opened his window to see, because wind's roar of the wind increased, and the reek kerosene of became overpowering. "You're good on the right," he said.

"Clear left," replied the left gunner as the helicopter slowly backed away from the tanker. The pilot reached up for the windshield wiper control and hesitated. If the windshield wiper motors so much as sparked, they would find themselves bathed in a fireball. He turned the dial and the milky veil parted, revealing towering peaks only a few miles ahead.

"We've got enough fuel," the right gunner said.

"Roger," the pilot responded. "Retract the probe, run the checklists, and let's get out of here. Pilot's controls, take a break."

The copilot relinquished the controls and shook her aching hands.

"Good job, Co," he added.

"Yeah, good job, ma'am," the right-gunner added.

"You didn't suck too bad," the left-gunner said. "I've seen worse. Hey, how about a little heat back here? I think the vomit is freezing on the floor. I'd hate to see someone slip and bust their ass."

As she reached up and turned on the heater, something warm trickled down her chin. She wiped it away and saw a dark smear on her glove.

The copilot tasted blood and realized she'd chewed the inside of her lip raw.

The sentinel on the tanker's ramp had vanished inside the

behemoth's belly, the cargo door now closed. The drogue retracted back into the pod as green flames brightened and lengthened from the tanker's engines. The airplane powered skyward, cleared the peaks and vanished into the starry heavens.

The pilot banked the helicopter hard right, and sliced down into the darkness. Skimming above the desert floor, the flying machine returned to its element.

The moment passed, but the mission had just begun.

Brian L. Braden is a retired U.S. Air Force pilot and intelligence officer. His articles have been featured in a variety of print and on-line publications and journals, including The Military Times *and* Air Power Journal. *Brian has published several books, including the epic fantasy novel* Black Sea Gods.

October's Daughter

By Brian Kerg
Third-Place Prose, 2018

From the Entry Control Point, I watched the sunset, a gush of evening's blood over the horizon. The flash of the sun on the Afghan mountain, miles distant, blazed like the gold of my daughter's hair. Both were just as unreachable.

I shook, more from reverie than from October's evening chill. Nangarhar Province gets cold fast, when the sun goes down.

Baddar, the Afghan soldier standing sentry at the ECP, looked at me. His dark eyes hid in an oak-brown face, lined with wrinkles as deep as bark. He was old enough to be my father. He said something to me in Pashtun, indecipherable. I threw back one of the few survival phrases I knew:

"*Sahr pikheyr*," I said. *Good morning.* I didn't know "good evening," but it was the best I had.

He said something again, and nodded with his head down the road, toward Bama'hel village, and the adjoining graveyard.

"I watched a funeral there, months ago," I said, pointing. "From our sentry tower. When your women wail in grief, it sounds like banshees. Spirits. Do you have ghosts, in Afghanistan?"

Baddar said something back to me in Pashtun, nodding again down the road. Perhaps beyond the graveyard and the village, all the way to the mountainside. Maybe he and I were reflecting on the same events.

"It reminded me of my little girl," I said. "The light on the mountainside. It's beautiful." She was beautiful, too.

Baddar nodded, grunting, as though agreeing. We watched the sunset, shivering together, able to say nothing to one another, saying all we needed to say. My radio crackled with static. I grabbed it from my cargo pocket, responding. "Calling station, this is Captain Graham. Say again your last, over."

"Sir, it's Gunny. The patrol's ready to brief. You still coming along tonight?" We were on our local net. Higher couldn't hear us, so Gunnery Sgt. Rikers wasn't going to waste time on radio protocol. I didn't know why I still wasted mine.

"Yeah. I'm *en route*." I took another look at the light on the mountain's side, now crimson and purple. The blood of armies from every age had consecrated these valleys and hills, splashed across mountains just like that. I shook my head.

"Later, Baddar," I said, nodding at the soldier. He grunted back at me, and I stalked back into our combat outpost.

The briefing room was a slipshod thing, just like the rest of our makeshift home we'd carved out of nothing in the middle of Nowhere, Afghanistan. Plywood and hope had kept the walls up during the thawing spring and the sweltering summer; with luck, it might live through the fall. All we needed it to do was make it to our rotation date, when we'd redeploy home and this corner of the graveyard of empires would be somebody else's problem.

A few sad Halloween decorations and hand-written letters were stapled to the wall; they'd been sent to us by some naïve classroom of second-graders, whose teacher thought she might invigorate our spirits with what we were missing back home. The centerpiece was a card drawn by Bobby Rogers, 8 years old, who'd sketched a giant pistol and the message in bubble letters: "HAVE A GOOD WAR." A stool in the corner had a plastic jack-o-lantern, full of the candy that the guys wouldn't eat, Mary Janes and Necco Wafers.

In the middle of the room was the sand table, a handmade topographical map depicting our battlespace, our own little slice of the Afghan pie for which we were responsible to secure along with our Afghan National Army counterparts. Half of our ANA brothers were ghost soldiers, existing only on paper so their commander could pocket their pay. I didn't mind these kinds of ghosts, anymore; they didn't haunt me.

In the center of the sand table was our combat outpost, our COP, surrounded by sloping valleys and hills, the Tora Bora Mountains to our east, a border police checkpoint, and a pair of roads and rivers.

One of the Marines had written "Trick or Treat!" in the top-left corner of the map, and added a crudely drawn penis. This was the art only my tribe could produce. These were the sons of America, my brothers-in-arms, sent forward to enforce *Pax Americana*. I wouldn't have had them any other way. Everyone in the platoon was gathered around the sand table, whether they were going on the patrol or not; if they were remaining behind, they were, by default, the Quick Reaction Force that would roll out if we got into anything heavy.

I looked at Gunny Rikers, and he nodded back at me, letting me know without a word that everyone was here.

I felt broken inside, a collection of jagged clay shards. But leaders can't be vulnerable, here if ever. Weakness is a deadly contagion. So I hid these pieces behind the mask of command, and aired the confidence my guys needed to see. It had been some time since I felt like the leader I could portray so well.

"Let's get started," I said, cutting through the idle chatter. The Marines quieted down and leaned forward.

"Tonight's going to be short and sweet. We're going to kick out along Road Blue, heading south to north from our COP up past Bama'hel village." I pointed with my finger as I briefed, indicating the route. "I want us to do a deliberate drive-by of the district governor's mansion, so he knows we're still running around at night, and he can let Kaiser Soze and his henchmen know it. The intent is to send the message that we're still being aggressive, even though they know we're out of here in a month and they don't try to get in one last hurrah before winter brings a halt to the fighting season."

We were a little unique in these parts. The Taliban wasn't the biggest threat we had to worry about. Our big fish was a local warlord we called Kaiser Soze, who ran a shadow government. His real name was Abdul Nafi, but as this underwhelming former schoolteacher was calling the shots in our backyard, the nickname we lifted from *The Usual Suspects* stuck. His men had launched a few harassing attacks against our COP. We'd been tasked to raid a few of his sites throughout our deployment, and had gotten ambushed once in turn. We'd added our own share of ghosts to this godforsaken corner of the world.

Some of the guys nodded, muttering agreeably. They knew this was something we needed to do. It was the next part I was worried about. I made eye contact again with Gunny, took a breath, and pressed on.

"After, we're going to break off from the road, and take Buttonhook Trail over to the river, clear the cache shacks one more time, and then take the long way back to the COP and call it a night. Any questions?" The guys were silent, and I knew they would be. We hadn't taken a patrol out that way since Baker died.

I looked around the room, to Gunny, and back at the guys. I sighed, gritted my teeth, felt the wall between me and the topic. That familiar wall, pushing back. We don't only wish to avoid speaking ill of the dead, we wish to avoid speaking of the dead at all.

"I'm going to talk right to it," I said. "Yeah. We lost Baker out there. But if we let the other team keep that ground, then the platoon that replaces us will lose their own Baker somewhere else, because the Kaiser thought we got complacent and thought he owned that space. We haven't kicked around in those huts for some time, and they might be using them for a weapons cache again. Tonight's about sending a message–a short one–and then we're back home. Can you give me a few hours to do this?"

A choppy chorus of "Yessir," followed, along with reluctant nods.

"OK," I said. "Then put on your costumes, gentlemen. Let's go trick-or-treating."

Our boots crunched on the rocky soil, but that noise was dulled by the howl of the wind shearing down the mountain and across the valley. We walked in a tactical column, in the dark, dispersed 10 to 15 feet apart. I looked at the patrolling figures through my monocular NVGs, and saw them in glowing shades of green, childhood ghosts from Disneyland's Haunted Mansion. I closed that eye, and looked through the other, using only my naked eye, and saw black silhouettes, armored Greek shades walking over ancient battlefields.

We passed the governor's house, the only 2-story structure in the valley, and posted security there for some time, the men taking a knee, making themselves visible to anyone watching. We knew the fat man was governor in name only, yielding to the pressure of Kaiser Soze. The Kaiser would be getting a phone call from the governor soon: the Americans are on the prowl, so make yourself scarce.

The wind howled, and I shook my head. A common saying here is that the Americans have all the watches, while the Afghans have all the time. They're right. They outlasted Alexander, the British, the Soviets. They'll outlast us, too.

I waved the men up, and we carried on. Buttonhook Trail looped hard east, sloping down toward the river. I sensed the patrol slowing as we approached the spot, and the collection of mud huts that marked the firefight where we'd lost Baker. I called another halt, and surveyed the area through my NVGs. The scene played out in my mind, a collection of bursting staccato moments, splices from a film edited from a nightmare.

We'd cleared the huts that day, found the weapons cache, confirming the intel provided by a local source, and were subsequently tasked to follow up on the alleged location of some of the Kaiser's men, across the river. We couldn't just drive our vehicles through the water, as we didn't know the depth. We'd have to ford it first, scouting for a route shallow enough where our vehicles could pass.

Baker was on point, taking careful steps in the river, the water nearly waist deep, gripping the rope he would have secured on the other end so the rest of us could make it with some ease. But water is relentlessly powerful, and always hungry, a devourer.

Shots started popping, like firecrackers, over Baker's head. We train our immediate action drills too well; he dropped the rope, and raised his weapon to shoot back. The river was hungry and strong. It swept him away and ate him up, the weight of his body armor and full magazines keeping him below the water's depths.

The attackers disappeared as quickly as Baker did, and the guys were denied the base satisfaction of a reciprocal killing. Our sister company, operating further down the river, were able to pull Baker's wet, drowned corpse from the river so we could box him up and send him home. We didn't see him again, though. The last we saw of him was when the river swallowed him whole.

My last sight of Baker, disappearing into the water, was eclipsed by the last sight of my daughter, slipping into the ocean deep.

A hand tapped on my shoulder, bringing me back to the present; Gunny Rikers. He gestured at his watch. I looked at my own. We'd been holding the security halt for 10 minutes.

Kicking myself, I gave the order to clear the huts. My Marines went in, cool, quiet, professional, like another drill in combat town back on Camp Pendleton. There were no dramatics, and nothing to find. No weapons, no garbage, or other signs of life.

I had the guys hole up there for a bit, munching on MRE snacks, and deliberately leave the trash and wrappers on the deck inside. If the Kaiser's men came back through, I wanted them to know we'd been here, and that we'd be back again. We'd contest the ground, and bloody his nose if we could, even if he did have all the time.

We hiked back to the COP, our hot breath steaming like dragon's fire in the night's chill.

The dream came again, as it always did, when I felt so exhausted I fooled myself into believing I'd luck into a good night's sleep.

My wife, my daughter, and I, on the beach in California. A military man with his buxom bride and beaming child, a regular Norman Rockwell painting, living the American dream. We baked, joyfully, in the sun's heat, building sand castles together. My little girl put seashells on the castle's top, crowning it with nature's turrets.

"I'll take her into the water for a minute," my wife said, wiping the sand on her bare thighs. Ex-wife, now, our marriage another victim to water's hunger.

I put my hand on my daughter's head, and ran it down her golden locks, kissing her on her baby-fat cheek. "Have fun, monkey," I said. She smiled at me. Her eyes were blue as the ocean.

I watched them wade into the water, my wife nearly waist deep, holding our daughter close. They started to swirl around in circles as the next tide rolled in, splashing. Both of them laughed, mad with joy, as wave after wave struck. I'll never forget how happy they looked.

A high wave hit hard, burying them both. My wife emerged, empty handed, her eyes white with terror.

A pounding awoke me. My heart was beating like a machine-gun. I fell out of my cot and reached for my flak jacket and rifle, assuming we were getting hit by more harassing fire.

"Sir? We need you." Gunny Rikers was knocking on my door.

"Yeah?" I said, clearing my voice, setting down my gear. Not an attack, then. He wouldn't beat around the bush if someone was trying to kill us. I glanced at my watch. It was 0500. If I was lucky, I could brew some coffee in our mess tent before the sun rose.

I shuffled across my room and opened the door. Gunny stood in the hallway of our wooden hut. He was in his brown fleece, green skivvy drawers, and black flip-flops. He looked as bleary eyed as I felt, grizzled and unshaved.

"You're never going to believe this," he said. His voice was a rumble of sifting gravel.

"Try me," I said, rubbing the sleep from my eyes with thumb and forefinger.

"Kaiser Soze's at our front gate," he said. "He wants to talk to you. He wants our help."

Kaiser Soze had tear-streaked cheeks and was covered in blood. He was a broken man. I could tell. We can recognize our own.

I thought you'd have to be taller, to be a warlord. Abdul Nafi– "Kaiser Soze"–was every bit as short and unbecoming as his namesake. He couldn't have been a buck-ten soaking wet, and he was soaking wet, having swam across the river to get to us. I stood head and shoulders above him. He looked even smaller as he stood there, shaking and shouting across the ECP at me and the men at my side. Two of my Marines had their weapons at the alert, buttstocks in their shoulders, ready to lift the muzzles and put rounds in the man if anything went sour, probably hoping it would so they could kill the man who'd caused Baker's death. Gunny Rikers made a point to stand midway between Abdul Nafi and the Marines, and remind them they weren't going to shoot anyone until they were told to.

Enzi, our Afghan terp, stood between me and the warlord. Enzi had turned his Atlanta Braves hat backwards on his head, and wiped sweat from his brow as he furiously interpreted back and forth between us.

"He says," Enzi began, his accent thin and sharp, "he and his men were overrun by Taliban. The new chief in this valley is Dava Jan, a young man, who says he is a warrior for God. They were not many but they came with surprise. Abdul tried to negotiate, but they wouldn't listen."

Abdul Nafi went on, gesticulating wildly with his hands. Enzi went pale, and started tugging at his scarf, his nervous habit.

"His men put down their weapons. They offered to join Dava Jan, to join the Taliban, but they were lined up against the wall and shot."

"Jesus," I said.

"Looks like our job out here just got easier," Gunny said.

The warlord muttered a few more lines, then collapsed to his knees, sobbing. "He says," Enzi said, swallowing a breath, taking his time, "they took his daughter. They will sell her off to be someone's bride. To Taliban strangers outside the tribe."

I took a long breath of my own. My hands on my hips, I surveyed the valley again, the looming mountain, glowering over us like a sentry, the village, and the graveyard, each marker just now visible in the pre-dawn gray. A light was on in the governor's house. A wide shadow was silhouetted in the second-story window, looking out toward us.

I crouched down, bringing my eyes level with Abdul's.

"How old is your daughter?" I asked.

Enzi translated. "Eight."

I swallowed back the hot bile rising in my throat.

"My daughter would have been eight this year, Abul Nafi," I said. "What is your daughter's name?" Again, Enzi asked the question in Pashtun.

"Sandara," he said.

"Sandara," I repeated. "That's a beautiful name. Tell him," I said to Enzi, keeping my eyes on Abdul Nafi, "tell him my daughter's name was Meadow."

Enzi told him. Still crying, and through Enzi, he told me, "That is also a beautiful name."

"Yeah," I said. "I know."

I brokered a deal.

Kaiser Soze, our long-running nemesis, would stay in the custody of my Marines at our COP. He'd bide his time here until we turned him over to our battalion intelligence section, when they could lock on a helicopter to fly out to us. Abul Nafi would tell us where to find Dava Jan. We'd strike now, while the iron was hot, while Dava Jan and his men might still be recovering from their raid against Abdul Nafi. And we'd try to bring his daughter back.

Gunny didn't like it, for many good reasons. The guys weren't keen on bargaining with the man who'd been trying to kill us for the last six months, and who'd helped put Baker in the ground. It wasn't directly in line with our mission on the ground either, to legitimize the local governor and build the people's faith in the Afghan national government. And, most likely, we were wasting our time. Most of these guys hit, then melt away. They likely wouldn't be there when we showed up. And Sandara, if she was still alive, was probably gone, too.

I could justify it, in a way. They always hit and run when they attack conventional forces like us, but don't have the same need to disappear when they're attacking other Afghans. An operational need was there, too–the Taliban would wrap themselves around the governor, just as

Abdul Nafi did. They probably already had their hooks in him, and I suspected the governor helped Dava Jan find Abdul Nafi and take his men by surprise.

Can something be selfish and righteous at the same time? I want to believe that, because I also believe all the men we'd kill and get killed in these hills and valleys wouldn't make a difference in the big picture. All the death and sacrifice would be lost to time's march. But we could do this one small, selfish, good thing, and light one votive candle in defiance of the void.

We were around the sand table again, ready for another briefing. I felt an anxiety and verve that had been lost to me since before my first deployment, when I was still naïve enough to believe that a few good men, with good intentions, could move the world in the right direction, when I was young enough to believe that my generation of volunteers could save the world from terrorism. It wasn't that long ago, but these few years of ruthless experience had aged me inside as though I'd been a lifelong smoker.

"OK guys, this is the big show. No more trading pot shots with Kaiser Soze, because we're holding him in a Quadcon out back and all his men are dead. Today we're taking it directly to a Taliban leader, Dava Jan, and his crew of about ten men."

As before, I oriented us to our location, gesturing at the sand table as I described the plan.

"We're here at the COP. Here's Bama'hel village. Across the river," I said, placing a few rocks on the map as markers, "is Landa'hel village. Kaiser Soze was hiding there in plain sight, expecting that we'd be keeping to our side of the river." Which we had. Under other circumstances, I'd be flagellating myself for submitting to that cowardice, but there was no time. "Our new Taliban playmates are there now, as they just massacred the old tenants so they could move in before the lease was up."

"We're going to roll out heavy, in MRAPs, up to the river. Gunners are going to provide overwatch, orienting guns north, drivers will stay on their wheels, while everyone else dismount to post security. I'll ford the river, making sure to find a spot that is shallow enough where our MRAPs won't get stuck."

Again, the room went deathly quiet. The guys were too professional to outright tell me they thought this part of my plan wasn't wholesome. Too many parallels with Baker.

"When I get to the other side, I'll secure my end of the rope in case anyone else needs to ford it on foot, but we should be able to mount back up and take the MRAPs over, one at a time. Then we drive to Landa'hel village. Two Vics will post up on this hillside as overwatch, and the rest of the vics will push into the village to support the search. We cordon and knock, house by house, until we get our man."

I threw a photo down on the sand table, a tall man with wiry, red-brown hair, a close-cropped beard, and hollow cheeks. "And this is our boy. He was already registered in the BATS database, with biometric data, photo, the whole shebang. He'd tried to volunteer with the Afghan Army a while back but got canned for preaching jihad during basic training. Take a good look."

I clapped my hands together for emphasis. "This is direct action, gentlemen. Kill or capture, with the hope of a rescue mission for added flair. It's the same *Call of Duty* bullshit that fooled us into signing up for this job in the first place. It's what we all really want to do."

A few nods, smirks, slaps on shoulders. "OK, guys. One last time outside the wire, *Insha'Allah*. Let's go wish our new friends a Happy Halloween."

We'd made it to the river. The MRAPs were posted just as I'd briefed, their hulking, metal frames providing a wall of shielding steel, their machine guns pointed, hunting, eager. The Marines had dismounted, formed a perimeter that was supposed to be focused on external threats, though half the guys were glancing, unsure, at me, as I stood at the bank of the river with one end of the rope in my hands, and the other tied to one of our vehicles.

I stared at the rolling water of the river. I saw Baker slipping beneath the surface, as though swallowed into a sinkhole. I saw Meadow snatched up in the grip of a wave and stolen away in a riptide. Saw the horrified mask of my ex-wife's face as she realized what she'd lost, and the agonized grief of Abdul Nafi as he wrestled over what he was going to lose.

I took off my Kevlar helmet and flak jacket, and dumped them on the ground. I handed my rifle to Gunny Rikers, then slipped off my desert combat shirt and stood there, bare-chest open to the sun and the breeze. I ran the rope through the loops on my belt, then again a couple of times around my stomach, and held the slack in one hand.

I started at the same place Baker did, five months ago, not for some redemptive purpose but because I knew he'd made it at least halfway across and stayed waist deep. Abdul Nafi couldn't recall where he'd crossed the river, only that he'd done it out of desperation and need.

I put one foot in the water. Immediately I felt the biting, wet cold. My teeth chattered as I took step after step, slowly sinking in until the water was at my belt.

I used my booted foot as a probe, feeling for the ground ahead of me before I committed to each step. My ankle nearly rolled on heavy rocks, and slipped on patches of pebbles and mud.

The sun, shining in the pale autumn sky, crisping my pale shoulders, was a burning contrast to the brown, murky, freezing water. A bird flew above me, eclipsing the sun, casting a shadow across my eyes like a shot as I stepped.

My foot found no purchase. I slipped, and felt the hand of the water grab and pull, greedy as a fairy-tale monster, and take me under.

The water crashed around me, biting, and I felt my muscles contract, trying to flee the paralyzing cold. The current pulled me downriver as my body tumbled deeper. I felt my bare shoulder scrape against rocks jutting out of the muddy bottom, slicing like knives. My bare head struck another rock.

Dazed, I opened my eyes in the water, tried to see through the dark and the mud. I felt the pull of the water, of cold limbs wrapped around my body, and saw in a flash the corpse-white arms and empty eye sockets of Baker, a vengeful ghost bringing me down to the river bottom to drown with him. I tumbled in the water, and my head struck bottom again. No, the arms were my daughter's, Meadow's. Not corpse-white but pink and lovely as the day she disappeared in the riptide, her eyes ocean blue. My lungs burned for air, my diaphragm pressed inside my chest like a squeezing fist.

As though another hand was wrapped around my waist, I felt myself being tugged in another direction. The rope around my waist; I was being pulled back and up. Two hands were on me, taking me opposite ways, like some beast trying to tear me asunder. I grabbed the rope, pulled, flailed my slow, heavy boots against any surface they could find to help bring me up. My right boot kicked a sloping wall. I lifted my foot, found purchase, stepped, felt a muscle strain as I pushed up.

I surfaced, gulping air, and tumbled to the left with momentum, almost falling over again. Shivering, I looked back, saw Gunny Rikers and two other Marines pulling on the taught rope. I was only a foot forward of where I'd gone under. Erosion and time had carved the sudden dip into which I'd fallen. Perhaps Baker was just stepping into it when he went under too. But one foot forward of this trap, the ground was solid, and without the weight of full kit, I wasn't doomed to drown in 4 feet of water.

Gunny shook his head at me and I could hear him swearing. Shivering, I took the rope again, and proceeded forward as before.

I made it to the distant end, collapsed to my knees, and bent my head to the ground, breathing, shivering, born again.

The MRAPs followed the path I'd set, tearing across the river with ease. Marines hammered green engineer stakes into that point to mark it for our way back, so we wouldn't drive over another unseen drop that would consign a vehicle and its passengers to the deep.

Toweled off, suited back up, I got back in my vehicle, and took the convoy into Landa'hel village. Its motley collection of huts was almost indistinguishable from Bama'hel village. As soon as we broke the cusp of the hill, villagers scrambled inside their huts, like townsfolk in a Western right before the big shootout. I was half-expecting a tumbleweed to blow across the road. Instead, we had only the lonely howl of the wind.

The guys executed just as we'd briefed. Two MRAPs posted on the hill overlooking the village. The rest of the MRAPs rolled down the only road and circled the wagons, surrounding the village. Marines dismounted. Half cordoned the first set of huts, weapons pointed inboard and outboard. The guys designated for the assault team followed me. I was making my way to the one house in the village with a blue door–Abdul Nafi's old house, the largest, the most grandiose with its meager status symbol of faded blue paint on a rotting wooden door.

The wall of the house opposite was clearly where Abdul's men had been executed. It was caked in splashes of red blood, flung across the door and the windows, like sacrificed Passover lambs used to ward off the angel of death. Did that make us emissaries of an avenging god? I hoped the blood couldn't bar us from our task, if we were.

I'd feared a long slough of a clearing drill, going house to house in the hunt for our man, who might have already slipped away like so many of the shadows we'd chased after before. We'd come up with nothing, having fallen into the insurgent's trap of terrorizing innocent families caught up in the latest instance of the war-torn history they'd inherited by the poor luck of being born to it.

But Dava Jan made it easy for us.

A burst of rifle fire exploded from the window of the house. We hit the deck as 7.62 rounds tore over our heads. The blue door burst open and three robed men ran out, bringing AK-47s up and firing wildly.

Lying in the prone, from stable positions, surrounding them, we had them outclassed and outgunned. The aggressors were cut down, almost ripped to pieces as the platoon shot back.

Gunny Rikers was already getting his squad up and stacked against one side of the house. Another fighter shoved his AK-47 outside the window inches from the squad and pulled the trigger, spraying and praying, hoping to hit a target. Gunny grabbed the shooter's wrists, wrestled him for a moment, then pulled violently in a wrestler's throw, yanking the man out of the window and slamming him to the ground.

He couldn't have been more than 15 years old.

The squad riddled the boy with fire and he stopped moving.

I tore my eyes away. I stood, and hurried my squad against the house. "Watch the windows!" I yelled.

Screams and shouting came from inside. A few men's voices. I thought I heard a child's cry, a girl's or a boy's, I couldn't tell.

Christ, I thought. We're going to kill her. If she's in there, we're going to kill her.

"Aim high!" I shouted. "Aim high, aim high!"

I lifted my weapon, and gave the signal for a man from my stack to breach. He nodded, rushed across the doorway, faced outboard from the blue door, donkey-kicked backward and lunged forward, clearing himself from the fatal funnel and the rounds that could follow him.

Weapon up, I stalked forward, and my stack of Marines followed.

As I turned into the plane of the door, I felt a dull, heavy thud against my flak jacket, as though I'd just been punched in the chest. I stopped my breach, felt the Marines behind press against me, stalled but heavy with momentum, still pushing forward.

I saw a tall, hollow-cheeked man, his hair in wild disarray, with murder in his eyes. Dava Jan.

He was looking down. I followed his gaze to the ground, and saw what had hit me.

The grenade rolled slightly in the dirt with what momentum remained. I thought it looked like a hatching egg.

There wasn't any time to backpedal. Instinct and training hijacked my body.

"Grenade!" I screamed as I started to stumble forward. I kicked it inside the house, caught myself on the door and slammed it shut as I was sandwiched between it and the Marines behind me, had a split-second to note the contrast of the dull, faded blue paint on the door with the brown of the mud walls.

For one agonizing second I realized what I'd done.

I held the door shut. I had to hold the door shut.

I felt, rather than heard, the concussive blast.

Disorientation, deafness, a high-pitched ringing. Mostly darkness, with shades of light. I was floating in an ether; mindless, without agency.

I remembered being a boy, after Sunday mass, lying under a tree in the garden beside St. Mary's church, watching the spring-bloomed limbs of a tree crisscross the path of the sun in a steady breeze, over and over, a beatific vision. I stayed there so long my back fell asleep, and I thought I was part of the ground. I thought that this is what death was like, or heaven, maybe. An endless moment of disassociated peace.

Then more sensation, a weight on my lungs, a dull pressure on my left side. A flash of light, exploding across my vision. Gunny Rikers ripping the exploded door off of my limp body. Another Marine slapping his hands across me, checking for wounds.

Coughing, I propped myself up, looked back through the doorway.

The rest of the Marines from my stack entered the house, finishing the assault, their shouts indecipherable through my tinnitus. A few dull pops as they put final rounds into the bodies of the men inside, ensuring they were dead.

I tried to get up, fell back down, face forward. I stared into the doorway, waiting to see a little girl walk out, a golden-haired, ocean-eyed seraphim, a beatific vision.

I held my breath in an endless moment, but felt no peace.

From the Entry Control Point, I watched the sunrise, a burst of morning life over the horizon.

Baddar stood next to me. We were both looking down the road, toward the village and the graveyard, watching the funeral. From this distance, the bereaved women, covered in blue hijabs, looked like phantoms. The men lowered the small corpse, covered in a white shroud, into a hole in the ground.

A light was on in the governor's house. A wide shadow was silhouetted in the second-story window, still looking out toward us, probably watching the funeral too.

Baddar said something, maybe to himself, maybe to me. It didn't matter.

I nodded back at him.

"Yeah, Baddar," I said. "I know."

Under armed guard and with zip-tied wrists, I'd let the Kaiser watch from the sentry tower at the other end of the COP. I didn't hear him crying. I wasn't going to turn and look. I didn't want to have to watch him break again. Not after what I'd done. Not when I was about to hand him off to battalion, where he'd disappear into some prison, somewhere, to be milked for intelligence and then forgotten about. I'd seen enough people get swallowed whole. I was tired of it.

I'd tried to light a votive candle, and burned my hand instead. At least the Kaiser got to see his daughter go in the ground. At least he'd know where to find her bones.

I lit two cigarettes, inhaling deeply from both, then handed one to Baddar. He took it without a word. We stood there, together, smoking, able to say nothing to one another, saying all we needed to say.

Brian Kerg is a writer and U.S. Marine Corps officer currently stationed in Norfolk, Virginia. He is a non-resident fellow at Marine Corps University's Brute Krulak Center for Innovation and Creativity. His fiction has appeared in such venues as The Deadly Writers Patrol, Line of Advance, *and the Veterans Writing Project's literary journal* O-Dark-Thirty. *His*

professional writing has appeared in such venues as War on the Rocks, Proceedings, The Marine Corps Gazette, *and* The Strategy Bridge.

No Rolling, Shrink

By Ryan Stovall
First-Place Poetry, 2018

I like you. You seem friendly enough, and
I've tried my damnedest to relate to you

the truth. For example, it's true I came
to you. But I came for pharmacy

and lethe, not because I want help rolling.
I can roll my own, thank you very much.

But some rocks never should be pushed aside,
no matter how long the cavern's fetid

contents have been left to lie and fester.
Some dark miracles are best left unseen.

Beyond my stone smolder unborn nightmares,
gravid memories, cold imaginings

–brothers buried, grave with my guilt and fear,
neurotic worries about my children,

cowardice, shame, and that nameless male lack
(call it unsatisfied animal lust)

that underlies a plethora of
human tragedies–all ultimately

reinforced by my complete and utter
decaying existential hopelessness …

Such are my antichristic afflictions,
and so are they so unsafely tombed. But

my weary, ribby, cart horse sense of self
preservation implores this pestilence

stay sealed up in darkness. No risk to you
if we should choose to press on with breathing

life into my dead, exposing them to
unkind light by my naming of their names.

Ryan Stovall is a former adventurer, world traveler, and U.S. Army Special Forces medic. His work has appeared in such venues as Rosebud, Geometry, The Cape Rock, Here Comes Everyone, *and many other small publications. Currently finishing his Master of Fine Arts degree with Fairfield University, Ryan lives near Bangor, Maine, with his wife and their too-numerous children.*

Maneuvering

By Colin W. Sargent
Second-Place Poetry, 2018

History remembers
The 1946 diplomatic mission President Truman
Took to South America aboard the *USS Missouri,*
Steaming out of Washington at midnight

    Into the stars

But might easily forget
The young man out here,

Slack, bony, and lank,
With red hair, maybe,
From Texas, maybe,
A young Navy lieutenant from the Piney Woods, then!
Maneuvering his destroyer
down the bulrushes of the Potomac
Softly as you'd tiptoe into your
Daughter's bedroom
To kiss her good night.

    God, it's dark out here

Dark as a Ouija board
Thrown down a mine shaft

And because the *Missouri* is as big
As Landover Mall and displaces
Most of the river, because

The president must be protected
Against all enemies, foreign and domestic,

Her destroyers must screen her

Far on the Maryland side,
Far on the Virginia side,
A bit dangerous, this screening,

Rushing into the blackness
With the bottom coming up quickly:

> *Like Braille the unseen shores*
> *sweep by, close enough*
> *to hear a Northern Spy*

Apple drop.

> *It was this dark*

The night he came back
late from hunting, and having shot nothing,
shot mistletoe from the tops of trees

for his little girls,

This dark the first time his captain,
old riverboat captain
who never would trust sonar,
whispered to him
near the shores of Leyte,

> *Take off your shoes,*
> *feel for the bottom*
> *with your stocking feet.*

And so at his command the entire watch section
aboard the *USS Dyess*
begins to take off their shoes,
calloused men
fresh from the Pacific Island War
strong enough to kick
your ass off the pier,

well these inexcorable toughs
are now shoeless and geisha sensitive

The mud quivering below
erogenous as custard,
dreaming of being touched.

How dark it is

Out here in the cattails
out here in the real world
where Washington's dollar probably splashed

And now these men are

Princess sensitive, vertiginous
waiting
waiting

geisha sensitive, opera appreciating

The quartermaster sighing
and lighting a cigarette.

"Many dark doorways
should only be entered
one man at a time," they say,

But here in the night
with all the stars in the jar

There is the kind of beauty
that simply embarrasses men

Night pouring in
and the bridge lit by heaven

Then a single tree in white

out in front of the rest

steps out on stage,
The universe inside out
laughing, like the abyss ...

Years later I ask him
Did you go aground?

And he smiles,
lights a pipe
beside the swimming pool
that a few months later
will be filling with leaves.

He's gone now
and I think of him,
one foot
in the darkness,
one foot

here
more ready than anyone
to sense this side
and the other side

And brave enough to go there before me.
I can't feel him beneath my feet.
I feel him ... everywhere.

Colin W. Sargent teaches writing at The College of William and Mary. A former CH-46D pilot and editor of the U.S. Navy's Approach *magazine, he started* Portland Monthly *in his home town of Portland, Maine in 1986, where he continues as editor and publisher. A Maine Individual Artist Fellow in poetry, and a graduate of the U.S. Naval Academy, he has a doctorate degree in creative writing from Lancaster University. His first novel,* Museum of Human Beings, *was published in 2008. His second,*

COLIN W. SARGENT

The Boston Castrato, *was published in 2016. He lives with his wife, Nancy, herself a former U.S. Navy officer, in Virginia and Maine. For more information, visit: www.colinwsargent.com.*

Inshallah Mañana

By Randy Brown
Third-Place Poetry, 2018

Señor Higareda taught us "*Ojalá*"
in seventh-grade *Español*, along with
our *hasta luegos* and our *hasta mañanas*,
some twenty-one years before the
Twin Towers fell, and still more before the day
that Saber2th slipped a well-intended "*Inshallah*"
into the end of an operations brief
7,000 miles from home.

Something clicked in that moment.
    Went off like a land mine.

"No! No '*Inshallah*!'" the Afghan officers lit up and
sputtered like fuzes at their men. "You! Will! Be! There! On! Time!"

Ojalá ... *Inshallah* ... Doesn't even matter
when we try to talk the same babble. Some things don't translate.

One man's wish
turns out to be another man's oath,

and yet another's promise
likely to be broken.

The best we can say is that each requires
a willing divinity, and a belief in tomorrow.
So help us, God.
Repita, por favor.

Randy Brown embedded with his former Iowa Army National Guard unit as a civilian journalist in Afghanistan, May-June 2011. A 20-year veteran with one overseas deployment, he subsequently authored the 2015 poetry collection Welcome to FOB Haiku: War Poems from Inside the Wire. *His poetry and non-fiction have appeared widely in literary print and on-line publications. A member of the Military Writers Guild, he co-edited along with Steve Leonard the 2019 anthology* Why We Write: Craft Essays in Writing War. He often blogs as "Charlie Sherpa."

.

2019

A Jeep to Quang Tri

By William R. Upton
First-Place Prose, 2019

"Fear lent wings to his feet." – *Virgil*

I have three memories of Quang Tri, Vietnam: One, it was the northernmost place I flew to in Vietnam, about 6 klicks from the North Vietnam border. Two, I was there less than 10 minutes. Three, it scared the crap out of me.

The day we flew to Quang Tri, you could have fried an egg on my forehead, it was that hot.

And it didn't matter if I was in the shade or in the direct sun. If I had been a wet sponge and somebody squeezed me I couldn't have sweated more. To make matters worse, the olive-green aluminum of the Caribou soaked up the sun turning the cabin and cockpit into a giant green furnace. The only refuge was 14,000 feet straight up, where the temperature averaged 50 degrees.

We had a brief respite from the heat on the 20-minute flight from Vung Tau to Saigon where we picked up our cargo. Lethargy nearly overcame me as I backed a Jeep and trailer into the oven-like body of the Caribou. After strapping it down and double-checking the plane for possible problems, Gray Tiger '99 was ready to go.

"Where we headed?" I asked Capt. Bracey.

"A small dirt strip near Quang Tri," he told me. "You'll enjoy this one, if you don't mind getting sandblasted."

"Sandblasted?"

"We're gonna fly in, drop the Jeep, and boogie out of there. It's a dirt strip with more VC than flies on a dog turd. Both engines stay running all the time. Sand, dust, gravel and shit from the prop wash will eat you up back there."

"So, what will you and Mister Stephens do while I'm eating sand?" I asked.

"Sip margaritas in the cockpit until you give the high sign. Seriously though, you won't have much time to unload that Jeep."

"You wouldn't leave without me, would you?" I asked.

Bracey avoided eye contact. "Not unless we had to," he said.

We flew out of Saigon at nine in the morning for the 4-hour flight. I laid back on the troop seats and put my mind to other things. I listened to Capt. Bracey and Mr. Stephens as they bantered over the intercom. I genuinely liked them. They had become my friends. I dozed off thinking of Myra Faye back home and the last night we had spent together. We were in the back seat of my '50 Dodge coupe and making out hot and heavy. Her hands had just found the zipper in my Levis ...

Click, click. "Wake up, Bill," Capt. Bracey said on the intercom. "It's crap-your-pants time. We're on approach to Quang Tri. Remember, at the end of the runway we'll turn around and stop. Engines running. Untie and off-load that Jeep. ASAP!"

"Roger, sir," I said.

"When you got it off, jump your ass back on board. Stay in contact. When you give the word, we're outta here. Move fast. You got that?"

"Got it, sir. You call someone to get the Jeep?"

"No can do," Capt. Bracey came back. "Mandatory radio silence."

"If no one's there?" I asked.

"Leave it and let's get the hell out."

"Got it," I said.

Through rear portholes, I checked the main landing gear for down and locked position. I went back to my regular seat in the front, sat down, fastened my seat belt and waited. Through a porthole on the starboard side, I saw the fiery streaks of tracer rounds as they whizzed by.

"Jesus. You see those tracers, Captain?" I asked

"Yeah! Looks hot down there! Got your flak jacket on?"

"I do now, and I'm sitting on the other one," I said.

"Good man. Those tracers might burn you a new asshole." I heard him chuckle nervously. "Thanks again for the steel butt plates you put under our seat cushions."

"Roger that, sir," I said. I watched out the portholes for VC. A flash of light. Another tracer. VC, for sure. I looked out a different port. A puff of smoke. Napalm? Maybe. I pulled my flak jacket tight. All I could think of was getting to the ground. Damned slow plane. Slow made an easy target to follow. Mother had been right. You could get shot out of the air. I looked out a porthole over my left shoulder. Still, a couple thousand feet off the ground. Another tracer. VC target practice.

The Caribou seesawed left-right, up-down as it fought the rising hot air currents. Capt. Bracey throttled the engines back to slow the plane even more. The nose dipped. I wanted to say, No! Speed up! Let's get on ground, drop that damned Jeep and get the hell out of there!

I turned against the pull of my extra-tight seat belt to look over my right shoulder. Movement below.

A flash. More VC? Ground fire? Another tracer? Shit, I couldn't tell. The jungle still lay a thousand feet below. Did Quang Tri have a runway? Would we crash into the trees? I pressed my mike switch and, trying to sound calm, asked Capt. Bracey, "Everything OK, Captain?"

Click-Click. He doubled-clicked his mike as an affirmative reply. I wished he would have talked. I looked into the cockpit. From the back, Capt. Bracey appeared intense, concentrated. Mr. Stephens was adjusting a dial on the instrument console.

I watched as Capt. Bracey pushed the throttle levers forward, then eased them back, the engines screaming, then groaning. Mr. Stephens pulled the flap control lever back. Hydraulic pumps whined, driving the flaps lower, slowing us even more. We were flying in slow motion. I felt like a plastic duck at a county fair waiting for some country sharpshooter to draw a bead. An airplane-sized bull's-eye.

Finally, I saw the straight border of the jungle clearing and the edge of the yellow, primitive runway in front of us. I heard a *Whap! Thunk!* at the rear of the plane.

"Holy shit, sir, We've been hit."

"You OK, Bill?" Mr. Stephens asked.

"I'm OK. Scared the crap out of me. Tail section took a round or two. Controls OK?"

He rocked the plane side to side. "Feels good," Capt. Bracey said.

Seconds later the main landing gear touched the dirt strip, sending up a cloud of yellow dust. An eternity later, the nosewheel touched down. I fumbled for my seat belt buckle. I couldn't find it. It had worked its way up under my flak jacket. My hands tore at the snaps holding the jacket together. I found the buckle, flipped it open, and stood.

The plane sped like a drag racer toward the end of the airstrip. I jumped to the Jeep trailer and bent down to undo the tie-down strap. *Damn.* The handle was on the other side. I scrambled across the cargo deck. As I pulled the strap over the trailer axle, it caught on something.

Nothing was going right. We'd never make it out of here.

I whipped the strap. Up and down. Up and down. It flew loose. I hustled to the front of the Jeep. Time had slowed to a near stop. I couldn't open the front strap's ratchet handle. My fingers disobeyed orders from my brain. The front tie-down finally let go.

Even with my fumbling, I had worked too fast. As Capt. Bracey reversed the props to help stop the Caribou, the Jeep rocked backwards, rolling slowly toward the cockpit. *Damn!* Had I remembered to set the parking brake? I jumped in the Jeep and pushed the brake pedal down with both feet as hard as I could. I pulled the parking brake handle. The Jeep swayed in opposite motion to the Caribou, but stopped moving.

When I heard the props return to normal, I ran to open the loading doors at the rear of the Caribou and pushed the toggle switch to raise the cargo door up and into the tail section. Another switch forced the ramp door down. Their small electric motors whined in unison.

"We're there, Chief," Mr. Stephens yelled. "As soon as I say, get that damned Jeep off."

"Roger, sir." From where I stood, at the open cargo door, I could look out without being seen. I saw nothing but the wall of vegetation that formed the perimeter of the landing strip. We had, it seemed, landed inside a huge square opening in a green salad.

Burnt avgas from the Caribou's engines now replaced the smell of fresh sweat that oozed from my body. My jungle fatigue jacket stuck to my skin. The plane lurched to a stop and Capt. Bracey pivoted her on the port landing gear to turn her around. The starboard engine roared, and the prop spun, slapping the air and throwing up a sandstorm of yellow dust.

We stopped. The engines settled into a coughing rhythm.

"Go, Bill," Mr. Stephens shouted.

I dragged the ramps down and put them in place. Rumbling engine exhaust noise dulled the usual clank of metal on metal. Particles of sand driven by fast turning propellers stung my face and splatted on my fatigues. I tried to forget the Viet Cong.

"Hold her steady, Captain, the ramps are on the ground."

"Roger," Capt. Bracey said. "Get a move on."

"I'm unhooking the intercom long enough to get this Jeep out," I told him.

"OK, Bill, get it done."

I jumped into the Jeep. Sunlight through the cockpit window shone on the Jeep's instrument panel.

The glare blinded me. Was that starter switch on the left or right of the instrument cluster? Sweat beaded on my hand and my fingers left wet streaks on control knobs as I groped. Moments passed before I found the switch and flicked it to start. The engine turned over and over and over. Panic!

I had done this a hundred times before and the engine had always started right away. I tried to remember the sequence for starting. Hit starter switch, pump gas pedal. I smelled raw gas. Carb flooded. I pushed the accelerator hard to the floor. Engine turning. It coughed. Blue smoke. Engine started. Rough, now smoother. I pulled the gearshift to first position. *G-G-G-Grind.* Stupid. Push the clutch pedal down.

First gear. Ease the clutch. The Jeep crept forward. Forward, tilt, down, off.

A figure ran from the dense jungle, handgun ready. Viet Cong! Shit! My gun was on the plane. I froze. No, too tall to be VC. Thank God! It was a camouflaged Green Beret. I exhaled in relief.

He looked at me, "Thanks, guy." His hand grabbed the edge of my flak jacket and pulled my stunned, unmoving body out of the Jeep. "Sorry," he said. "In a hurry." He stepped into the Jeep, roared off, and disappeared into the foliage.

I tossed the ramps into the cargo bay. They left huge gouges in the wood decking. I didn't care. I jumped into the plane and closed the ramp door. The cargo door was still up, no matter. I sat down and hooked in my headset. *Blat-blat-blat.* Small arms fire.

"Ready, sir. Let's get the hell out of here." My uniform dripped with sweat. I fastened my seat belt.

"You got it," Capt. Bracey said. I watched his hand push the throttles as far forward as he could.

The twin engines screamed and strained as the props cut through the hot, heavy air. The plane crept forward before picking up speed. It shook and shuddered as if trying to jump off the ground. From where I sat in the back of the plane, I watched through the open cargo door for VC. The flak jacket I usually sat on had slid off my regular seat up front. It lay on the floor now. Fifteen feet away. I wondered what it would feel like to get shot in the butt.

Through the port across from me I watched the main gear tires roll. One revolution, two revolutions. Three, four, five, faster, faster. We sped toward the end of the runway until that momentary feeling of weightlessness as we lifted off. Inertia tugged the untied loading ramps back to the ramp door much like the dead mayor's coffin on my first mission. Screw it, if they slid out, that was just too bad. The jungle shrank behind us. We climbed. Higher and higher. The hydraulic pumps groaned once again as the flaps rose. Then the landing gear doors closed with a soft thud.

"Gear up, sir."

"Thanks, Chief, you done good."

"I thought we'd never get out of there," I said.

"It took us 30 seconds from power-up to wheels-up," Mr. Stephens announced. "Just 3 minutes from landing to takeoff."

"Any more tracers, Captain?" I asked.

"Didn't see any," Capt. Bracey said. "The VC must've wanted that Jeep more than they wanted us."

When I was able to stand, I went back to the tail section, dropped the cargo door into place and looked up. I saw a small hole on the tail's port side and a larger ragged hole high on the starboard side. A pointed piece of sheet metal flapped in the upper opening. No cables or control rods had been damaged. We seemed to be all right.

I resumed my place at the front of the Caribou. "No big deal on that hit," I told both pilots. "Only sheet metal work."

"Great, Bill, How you doin'?" Capt. Bracey asked.

"I'm OK, 'cept for the smell."

"What smell?" Mr. Stephens asked.

"I think I crapped my pants," I said.

"Me, too," said Mr. Stephens.

"Me, too," said Capt. Bracey. "Anyway, good job."

"Roger that, Captain," I said.

On the way back to Vung Tau, I wrote home:

Dear Mother and all,

I thought I'd write before you cut me out of your will. Not much going on here, and boy, is it hot. Only 150 days to go and I'll be home. I've *changed my allotment to $250 each payday. By the way, have you heard from Myra Faye recently? Would you call and find out if she's all right?*

We flew to Quang Tri today. That's about as far north as you can go in South Vietnam. We delivered a Jeep. No big deal.

I'll tell you about it when I get home. Well, I just wanted you to know that I'm still kicking. I'll write again as soon as I can.

– Your Loving Son,
Bill

At age 17, Vietnam veteran, William R. "Bill" Upton, enlisted in the U.S. Army in 1963. During his 5-year military stint, Upton completed his high-school training and was awarded a GED certificate. He served at many duty stations, including one year in Korea, and another as a fixed-wing CV-2B "Caribou" crew chief in Vietnam. For his wartime service, he was awarded the Air Medal and presented a certificate of achievement by Gen. William Westmoreland.

After leaving the Army as a sergeant E-5, he studied at Linn Benton Community College in Albany, Oregon and later Linfield University in McMinnville, Oregon, where he graduated cum laude *with an undergraduate degree in liberal studies. His writing has appeared in literary journals and magazines. His memoir,* Pizza & Mortars: Ba-muoi-ba and Bodybags, *was published in 2004.*
Upton is married to artist and retired educator Susan Upton. They live full-time in Sarasota, Florida and spend much free time with children and grandchildren in Oregon and North Carolina.

American Spirit

By Brian Kerg
Second-Place Prose, 2019

I was digging a pack of American Spirit out of my pocket when he came out onto the smoke deck. He was young and lean but his eyes looked as old as the sea. A nice surprise; I didn't think I'd find my type underway. And cliché or not, every sailor has a soft spot for Marines.

A gust of wind off the West Pacific snatched the smokes from my hand. Quick as lightning, he leapt forward and caught the pack. He didn't know it, but I was in his palm, easy as that. He handed me back my smokes.

"Mind if I bum a loosie?" he asked.

I shook one out of the pack, lit it up, and passed it to him before lighting one for myself.

"Sarah," I said, all the introduction he needed.

"Mike," he replied, and took a long drag on his cigarette. "A pleasure," he said, exhaling.

We puffed in silence, leaning on the rails, watching the ship's wake, a long trail to the horizon, marking the way back home.

"You know," he said, "I always thought it was unseemly. To see a woman smoking."

"Funny," I said. "I was going to tell you the same thing."

He grinned. And just like that, he was in my palm, too.

The claxon wailed in panicked alert, and the voice of God cried out over the mass communication system, summoning the Visit, Board, Search, and Seizure team. We had a suspicious contact to our starboard bow and my sailors and I had to go take a look.

"You'll have to excuse me," I said, taking one last drag. I tossed the cigarette overboard, sending an arcing spiral of smoke over the sea, like ghosts of sailors lost at sea, trapped in Davey Jones' locker. "Duty calls."

"Wait," Mike said. "Where do I find you?"

"It's a ship," I said. "You'll find me."

And he did, of course. Even if our time was fleeting. Watch officers know no rest.

But we always found each other on the smoke deck. And we grew closer, there, than we might have been able to in any dive bar or apartment back home.

We'd been underway nearly two months without a port call, and I was running low on my smokes. In the spirit of rationing, I was sharing mine with Mike, taking a puff and passing it along. I could taste him on the cigarette, relished it, knew he relished my taste, too; when it's against the law to consummate a relationship at sea, you have to work with what you've got.

"So what's happening with you?" he asked. "After this deployment?"

"Burning all my leave," I said. "Going to tear it up all across wine country. Try to forget I'm in the goddamn Navy and that the end of this float only means I get to train for the next one. How about you?"

The wind caught a hair, pulled it loose from my bun. He risked a touch, tucked it back behind my ear.

"Burning all my leave," he said. "Try to forget I'm in the Marine Corps. And try not to think about where my battalion is going next. It's not another float."

We didn't say anything for awhile, and simply stared at the wake instead. Too much talk about the future was exquisitely awful. The ugly inconvenience of more deployments, and of wars most of the country had forgotten, and what they could mean for me, and Mike, and any hope for what we might have when we had dry land under our feet again, was harrowing.

Mike did us the favor of turning our thoughts back to the present and the joy, however fleeting, it brought us.

"But if it's up to me, I'll take the sea over the desert."

"Why's that?"

He looked me up and down. "Better company."

The claxon wailed, another call for tribute, this time for an air assault drill.

"My turn, this time," Mike said. "I get to play dead weight inside of an Osprey."

He pulled his hand back to throw the cigarette overboard. I caught his wrist.

"Come with me," I said. My voice cracked, a traitor, belying the need for him that grew like a seed in the pit of my stomach.

"Where?"

"Wine country," I said. "When we get home."

"It's a date," he said, grinning. I plucked the cigarette from his hand

and he trotted off to kit up and head to the bird. I finished the smoke, savoring the taste of his lips, the closest thing to a kiss he could give me.

I was on the bridge when the Osprey went down. I was one of the first to know there was no way Mike could have survived. The sea was hungry and chewed up the Osprey like the foil on an Easter chocolate. The debris from the crash put up an arcing spiral of smoke off the sea, like a burnt offering to a pagan god. Everyone on board died. We never found Mike's body.

After we got back to the States, I still went to wine country. I wore a sun dress and dolled myself up every day, took drives along the coast with the top down and my hair up, an homage to Audrey Hepburn, the woman I wanted to be for a man of my own like Mike.

I thought the tears would come when the sun went down and the wine flowed like water, or with the agonized hangovers that bit like a crown of thorns. But real tears need a heart, and mine was at the bottom of the sea, locked up tight in Davy Jones' locker. So instead I cling to all I have left, the ugly inconvenience of another deployment and a pack of American Spirit, and I try to taste Mike's lips on my cigarette as I hold it in my mouth.

Brian Kerg is a writer and U.S. Marine Corps officer currently stationed in Norfolk, Virginia. He is a non-resident fellow at Marine Corps University's Brute Krulak Center for Innovation and Creativity. His fiction has appeared in such venues as The Deadly Writers Patrol, Line of Advance, *and the Veterans Writing Project's literary journal* O-Dark-Thirty. *His professional writing has appeared in such venues as* War on the Rocks, Proceedings, The Marine Corps Gazette, *and* The Strategy Bridge.

Rocks for Breakfast

By Travis Klempan

Third-Place Prose, 2019

27 March 2007

"That Harper Lee," Mack said, "is full of shit."

A group of green Army 5-ton trucks–three functional vehicles perched around a fourth with its hood open–had disgorged the few dozen members of 2nd Platoon, Charlie Company, 1st Battalion, 33rd Infantry Regiment into a Dunkin' Donuts parking lot. The soldiers waited with varying degrees of patience in the rising Georgia sun.

Sergeant John Mackenzie watched as several men hovered around the engine compartment of the broken truck. Two soldiers from Second Platoon were shade tree mechanics and had offered the Base Motor Pool contractor their pointed and conflicting opinions on the source of trouble. A fourth man–a local on his way to work, bib overalls and trucker hat hinting at his profession–had pulled over and spat a stream of tobacco onto the asphalt, proposing to fix the truck for free so long as they killed him some ragheads when they got where they was going even if they couldn't say where he understood.

Mackenzie smirked. He'd written that phrase down, though he wasn't sure what to do with it.

A fifth man stood slightly apart from the cluster, a cell phone pressed to his ear ever since they'd pulled over. An hour gone by and the truck still sat useless. Mack turned from the vehicles back to the task at hand.

"How's that now?" Staff Sergeant Julius Atwood craned his head as he chucked a pebble at a near-full green dumpster.

"Shouldn't you be over helping the lieutenant?" Mack smiled.

Atwood shrugged and lobbed another pebble at the trash heap. "I told him. Said he should just requisition us a school bus from Motor Pool, get our happy asses back on the trail. Have ourselves a more comfortable ride that way, too." He looked over at the dead truck. "LT said Kujo was real keen on the battalion all rolling out together, World War II-style, all jumping off the 5-tons and running around and rendezvousing at the airfield." He laughed. "That man's been watching too much *Band of Brothers.*"

"Rendezvous? Airfield? He really say all that, Gus?" Mackenzie held a small rock in his hand but didn't throw it.

Atwood shrugged again. "Who? Lieutenant Cruz? Colonel Kujo? I offered my two-cents'. Give him another 10 minutes and if we don't got a working truck I'll offer another two cents', slight more forceful even." He smiled. "Anyway, Knife, what'd you say about Harper Who?"

Mackenzie looked at the overflowing dumpster. A small gang of mockingbirds picked through the trash–greasy wrappers, coffee cups, half-eaten remains from yesterday's business–and scattered the debris onto the asphalt. Atwood had been throwing pebbles for the past few minutes, Mack and the birds his only audience. Ping and the birds went flying; few seconds later they returned. Not much of a game, but both men knew that killing time was a skill the Army didn't teach in Basic Training, least not outright.

Mackenzie scanned the parking lot. Small knots of soldiers were killing time, or trying to. The trick, he'd figured years back, was to engage in something requiring a minimum of physical and mental effort without sacrificing the last shreds of readiness. Playing cards was too mentally demanding; smoking not demanding enough. You could combine activities–dip tobacco and try to spit at something, for instance. Toes of other men's boots were good targets. Bugs in motion offered a challenge. Napping defeated the whole purpose, and it was way too early in the deployment to crack open a book.

He glanced down at his rucksack, saw the rectangular blocks of stories pressing against the green fabric. He and Atwood had set their rucks up against concrete parking blocks as soon as Lt. Cruz had declined Atwood's advice. The LT was the LT, and the platoon sergeant was the platoon sergeant, and Sgt. Mackenzie was Mack the Knife, but by the end of the day they'd all get to the airport one way or another.

"Airfield," whatever. Mackenzie smiled. Kujo had a hard-on for all that Patton-shit.

"Harper Lee, man. You actually are from the South, right? You did go to a school once, didn't you? She wrote *To Kill a Mockingbird,*" he said, rolling the pebbles in his hand like dice. "You know–classic of American literature? Wrote a classic, said she was done? Anyway, she says in it, talks about how killing a mockingbird's a sin, because all they do is sing their hearts out." He pointed at the dumpster. "All I seen them do is rat-fuck garbage cans looking for leftovers."

Atwood laughed, a short soft bark. "Just remember to be easy with that swearing. You know the LT is keen on polite language."

Mackenzie nodded. "Yeah, figure he's gotta have some sort of tic to define him. Leadership and all that."

Atwood stopped throwing rocks. They turned and watched the lieutenant, cell phone pressed to his ear and pacing, then turned back to the dumpster. Atwood dropped the pebbles from his hand and wiped his palms together.

"Birds just getting their breakfast, right?"

Mackenzie shrugged.

Atwood grinned and looked directly in Mack's face. "C'mon Knife, what're they saying?" His head remained still but his eyes darted over to the dumpster.

Mackenzie sighed. "I told you. It don't work like that."

A young man walked up and stopped a few feet short. "Staff Sgt. Atwood?"

"What is it, Nuñez?"

Private Nuñez rubbed his hands on his trousers. "Well, sergeant, me and some of the guys, we were wondering if you knew when we're getting outta here."

Atwood smiled and Mackenzie sensed what was coming. He looked at his feet.

"Yeah? Why's that? You fellas got appointments to keep?"

"Uh, no, sergeant, we just–"

"You getting bored? Want me to think up something y'all can do to kill time?"

"Not really, Sarge, I–"

"Think the rest of the battalion gonna leave us behind? They get to Iraq before we do, win the war without us? Think we'll miss the victory parade they gonna throw?"

Mackenzie ducked his chin to his chest to hide his smile.

"No, Sarge, we were just wondering–"

"Wondering is for officers, Nuñez," Atwood said. Mack looked up. Atwood played his role better than anyone else in the battalion. Tough, strict, but no voice for malice. "The LT's got his LT-stuff to do, us sergeants got our sergeant-stuff to do, and you privates have your private-stuff to do, and sometimes we all have the same thing to do, and that's just 'Hurry Up and Wait.' Hooah?"

Nuñez waited for a moment and nodded. "Hooah, Sarge." He turned, walked to a group of soldiers standing at the edge of the lot.

Mackenzie tossed a rock but not at the dumpster. "Hurry Up and Wait." He smiled. "Closest thing to a commandment I think I can believe in."

Atwood looked at him, then at Nuñez and the others and pointed. "Birthplace of rumors right there, all them privates in one place," he said. "Course that's a commandment. Got more truth than anything else in this line of work."

Hurry Up and Wait. Mackenzie considered the inevitability and implacability of the maxim, the combination of dread resignation and heart-pounding anticipation bound up in the four words. He wondered if it had ever been cliché or instead been born with truth in its teeth.

"You think the Minutemen had to Hurry Up and Wait before they saw the whites of the British eyes?" Atwood asked.

Mackenzie nodded. "Sure as shit the Spartans Hurried Up and Waited on the Persians." He laughed.

"Hell, even cavemen probably had grunts, say the same thing, when they were waiting on a brontosaurus or whatever." Atwood glanced at Mack, who kept silent. "Ugh."

A slow-burning truism at once reassuring in its consistency and upsetting in its indifference to the plight of mortals. No matter the meticulousness of the planning–and often in some perversely inverse correlation to the amount of forethought–something could, always did go wrong. The key was in knowing that, and anticipating how to kill the time once it arrived.

Mack finally laughed.

"What?"

He turned to Atwood. "What if Nuñez were right, Gus? What if the battalion did end up leaving us behind?"

Atwood shook his head and frowned. A couple hours wasted on the asphalt in Georgia could translate into a day lost by the time they changed planes in Germany, could cascade into a week behind in Kuwait, could mean a whole month gone before they caught up to the battalion in Irbil.

"Fat chance that happens," Atwood said, a smile breaking through.

"Yeah, but think, they could get there so far ahead of us they might actually win the war before we arrive."

"Even fatter chance that happens." Atwood stooped and picked up a pebble. "Without Second Platoon Charlie around they'd be lost." He grinned, white teeth flashing against his skin. "Even with us, how's anyone gonna win this one?" He tossed the rock, skipping it off the asphalt, into the side of the dumpster. "This ain't one for winning."

"Then what's it for?"

Atwood locked eyes with Mackenzie. "You know. Surviving. Keep the men alive best we can, get us all back one piece best we can." He turned to the birds. "Then we all go back to what we do, what comes natural. Nuñez, the LT, you, me, Colonel Kujo, the Iraqis, them mockingbirds–" He cut himself off with sudden laughter. "What you figure they ate before we invented dumpsters?"

Mackenzie laughed along with Atwood. "I read that coyotes are one of the only animals that did better once white men closed the frontier. Never died off, learned to eat garbage and poodles and they just kept multiplying."

Atwood nodded. "Makes sense it wouldn't be something majestic, like a buffalo. A bear. Had to be coyotes."

"Coyotes are OK. They're survivors."

Atwood nodded. "Couple more years there won't be nothing left but coyotes and mockingbirds. Rats, too. Cockroaches and pigeons."

"Won't that make for a zoo?"

The men turned their heads in unison at the sound of an engine coughing to life.

"Hell of a zoo," Atwood said, dropping his handful of rocks.

"Fuck you guys."

"C'mon, Nuñez, they don't care." Alphabet closed his eyes and leaned back as the truck bounced down the Georgia highway, their bodies rocking up and down.

Nuñez shook his head. "Now I look like a whiny bitch."

"And yet, you're still whining." Stevenson grinned across the truck.

"Like I got all the questions."

Alphabet laughed. "No sweat. Not like they got all the answers."

Greeble elbowed Nuñez. "But you listen to them just the same, hear?" His face loomed close behind the jab and Nuñez recoiled from his acne and lisp. The bodies crammed in to the back of the truck made pulling away difficult.

"Whatever man, so they been over there and come back couple of times. Lots of guys been over there and come back." He shifted in his seat. "I get Atwood, he's the platoon sergeant. What's Sgt. Mackenzie supposed to be? No other platoon's got an extra sergeant just floating around."

"He's a fucking expert's what he is," Alphabet said, dropping his smile. "One of the smartest guys in the battalion. He don't say much but it's worth hearing."

"What he says? He's always spouting off some weird voodoo hippie bullshit, Buddhist riddles. Like he talks to birds and shit. I don't understand him half the time."

"Well, the half you do understand, you best follow." Cristobal, one of the Team Leaders, a two-time deployer, leaned in. Alphabet was also a Team Leader, but only had one deployment. "And it ain't Buddhist riddles. Man's actually a Buddhist, I hear."

Greeble smirked. "The hell? Ain't Buddhists pacifists?"

Cristobal shrugged and leaned back. "I heard he's never fired his weapon, except at the range."

Nuñez smiled, baring his teeth. "How's he get away with that?"

Cristobal shrugged. "I heard he was just a dumb private in 2003, same as you dopes now, when his whole squad got wiped out going over The Berm. Hooked up with some guys from Third ID, tagged along for the Thunder Run. In '05, he led his squad through the Mother of All Firefights in Ramadi, brought all 12 guys back. Did it all without discharging his weapon once."

Greeble chuckled. "Yeah, but don't they call him The Knife because–"

Cristobal cut him off with a look. "You wanna know, you ask him. Don't ask me."

Stevenson nodded along. "Atwood's even crazier, see? During the invasion, he went head to head with a Republican Guard tank platoon in a Bradley. Somehow killed three tanks and sent the rest running. Came out of that one with all his nuts intact. He was there two years ago in Fallujah when shit got real bad, got his men through and back."

Nuñez grunted. "Heroes, then."

Stevenson shook his head. "Nope. Just really lucky fuckers."

❖ ❖ ❖

28 March 2007

"Wake up."

"But we'll never make it to the Super Bowl."

"Jaime, wake up."

Second Lt. Jaime Bustamante Cruz knocked the tray table with his knees, spilling books to the cabin floor. He blinked his eyes, dry and itchy, until he could focus on Tall Paul Berry seated next to him.

"I'm awake." He glanced out the oval window, dim dawn spilling in. Vague green shapes and patterns below–land? How long asleep? "I'm awake." He contorted his body, collected the papers, books at his feet. Tall Paul handed a photograph to Cruz.

"That your old man?"

Cruz looked at the makeshift bookmark. A young man stared back across years, eyes fierce. Buzz cut contrasted with a 3-day beard. The man skinny, skinnier than Jaime ever saw him in real flesh. Then-1st Lt. Tomás Esteban Bustamante wore faded green pants and a pale bandage over one ear. Rifle over his naked shoulders.

"Vietnam, '66." He yawned, stretched, reaching for the bottle of water in the seatback pocket. Empty. Recycled air, cool as a New Mexico morning but somehow drier. When had he finished the water? Last night? Over the ocean? What day was it anymore? "His second tour." He shook his head and rubbed the heel of one hand in his eyes to clear the fuzz. "What's up?"

"Man-zilla just stormed through here." Cruz looked toward the voice coming over the top of the seat in front. Small Paul Capuano peered at Cruz, eyes and nose visible, hideous mustache–within regulations, but still the target of the company commander's ire–hidden behind the seat. "Captain was worked up. Something about rumors coming through the cockpit."

Cruz looked at Tall Paul. "Rumors of what?"

Shrug. "Going to Irbil might be off the table. Going anywhere in Kurdistan is probably off the table. Evidently some battalions got caught up in the Surge, had to rotate early out of the east to cover a rougher-than-expected patch of Baghdad. Since the north is pretty quiet we may be getting sent to cover part of Diyala Province."

Cruz leaned back into his seat. "Awful lot of detail for just one rumor." Looked at the stacks of papers and books. Since reporting to

1st Battalion, 33rd Infantry, he'd spent most of his time cramming. Printed out and marked up hundreds of pages of Lessons-Learned, After-Action Reports, Significant Activities, State Department briefings; purchased a half-dozen books covering Islam, Sunnis and Shiites, the Kurds, the history of the Middle East, Iraq, Iran; days and nights of highlighting, note-taking, rereading spent in preparation for a mission to Kurdistan, the semi-autonomous northern portion of Iraq, partnering with and training of the Kurdish security forces, the peshmerga.

Two weeks ago Major Eichelberger, the executive officer, described their assignment to the officers of the battalion as "glorified parade duty."

The north was safer than the rest of the country, safer even than parts of America. It was far from the Sunni Triangle and Sadr City, from the sectarian fault lines running through the capital, outside the Iranian sphere of influence. The *Peshmerga* had a reputation as capable, professional soldiers, unlike the New Iraqi Army and the Iraqi National Police. The north was mountainous, far greener, bordered Turkey and Iran ...

Cruz consulted his notes. Did he know anything about Diyala Province?

"Buddy of mine from West Point deployed there last year," Small Paul chirped from behind his seat. "Just started turning into a shit show when he rotated out. Mortars, rockets, IEDs, suicide bombers, standup firefights, snipers ..." Cruz couldn't tell if Small Paul was smiling or frowning.

"But no official word yet?" Cruz asked, his cottony mouth demanding a stewardess with a pitcher. Lieutenants Tall Paul and Small Paul had led 1st and 3rd Platoons respective for near three months, eternities next to Cruz and his six weeks. They had nicknames, mostly to distinguish the two Pauls in conversation, as did their platoons–1st Platoon's "Fireballs" and 3rd Platoon's "Death-Dealers."

Cruz didn't need a nickname for himself but wanted one for 2nd Platoon, something fierce but not profane. One thing he'd made clear to his platoon sergeant and the men was a low tolerance for profanity. They at least avoided the F-word in his presence. He was still working on the lesser curse words.

Tall Paul shook his head. "This all came down like two minutes ago." He leaned into the aisle and looked toward the front of the plane. "Man-zilla seemed pretty amped, though. I'd imagine Kujo is even more worked up."

"Man-zilla always seems amped," Small Paul pointed out. "And Kujo–"

"Well," Cruz said. "I'm going to see if my sergeants are awake. We must be getting close to Germany by now either way. No spreading rumors, least not in Second Platoon." He stood and squeezed past Tall Paul. As he stepped into the aisle Cruz realized they'd whispered their entire conversation.

His sergeants appeared in the aisle as if summoned. Staff Sgt. Atwood, his platoon sergeant, and Sgt. Mackenzie, his ... other sergeant. Still didn't know what to make of the man. Something about him rubbed Cruz in a way not quite wrong, just uncomfortable.

"Diyala, sir?" Atwood usually ignored small talk so Cruz just nodded.

"Nothing official yet," he admitted, lips pressed tight into a line. "I only just heard from the company commander." Wasn't exactly a lie, was it? "Until we get further word from Capt. Manzanillo I think we just make sure the men are up and getting what they need. Smokes will have to wait until we're on the ground in Germany. In the meantime, water, snacks, coffee." He offered Atwood a smile. "Make sure you get some for yourself, Sergeant."

Atwood nodded emphatically. "Damn right, sir." He marched off in search of a stewardess and a pot.

Cruz looked at his extra sergeant. A cipher. Two combat deployments, alongside Atwood's two, and a number of men in the platoon and the company and the battalion with multiple deployments, all while Cruz had been biding his time in college, summer internships and road trips and semesters spent cramming for engineering finals. At least the two Pauls were first-timers, too.

Cruz gave Mackenzie the same brief smile he'd given Atwood.

"This is your third time over, Sergeant?" Mackenzie nodded. "Well, third time's the charm, right?"

Mack shrugged. "Or bad things come in threes, sir." He nodded curtly and went off in Atwood's wake.

"Fucking Mackenzie." Cruz shook his head. "Damn Mackenzie."

Lt. Col. David Kujarowicz looked around the small room. It was the best the XO could do on short notice, but this was not the sort of martial background Kujo had ever envisioned for leading men to war.

He kept his face impassive. He wondered what General Patton would've said if he'd had to make his grandiose speeches from an airport lounge. He grunted. Damn sure the man would've laughed at doing it in a *German* airport lounge, Kujo thought.

"Sir?" Major Eichelberger leaned close, his quiet voice even softer with anticipation. "The officers are all here, along with most of the NCOs."

Kujo nodded. "Thanks, Karl." He cracked his giant knuckles and tried to meet each man's eyes. "Men." He offered a tight grim smile. "Sure by now you've heard rumors. Since the cat's out of the bag we might as well skin it. Kurdistan is out. We are headed to Diyala Province." He waited, wondering if there'd be mutters or murmurs. There weren't, so he continued. "As some of you may know, Diyala is to the east of Baghdad." He nodded at that fact. "It's also a lot more dangerous than Kurdistan, but all that really means is we'll get more opportunities to do what our Army and our taxpayers have asked us to do: 'close with, engage, and destroy the enemy.'" He would have paced the room but the combination of tight confines and numerous bodies prevented him. "Since the Army says we aren't technically prepared for Diyala we'll be getting an extra two days in Kuwait to requisition additional gear and acclimate the men."

Kujo swore he heard a groan.

"We'll be posted to Forward Operating Base Dillinger, co-located with the State Department Provincial Reconstruction Team, and a battalion slated to depart in a few months. Make sure you use that time to get with your counterparts and learn everything you can. When they leave, it'll be just us for the next 15 months."

A hand rose in the back. Kujo squinted at Capt. Manzanillo from Charlie Company. "Yes, what is it, Hector?"

The younger man leaned forward. "Fifteen, sir?"

Kujo nodded. "That's the other change. We've got two additional months in Iraq to show what kind of professionals we really are. Sixty more days." He glared around the room, daring anyone else to groan. "I know these are large and last-minute changes. Some of your men may complain. But the United States Government, the United States Army, and most importantly the American people have invested millions of dollars towards reconstituting, training, and equipping this battalion. We now have a chance to go out and make an immediate difference, not just sit on our duffs in Irbil training some militiamen to do traffic stops and baggage checks. Diyala will undoubtedly prove a much more difficult mission, perhaps more dangerous, but we all know Rome wasn't burnt in a day."

Travis Klempan was born and raised in Colorado. He joined the U.S. Navy to see the world. After realizing most of it is water, he returned to the Mile High state, collecting degrees in English, creative writing, and ethics along the way. He is the author of the 2020 novel Have Birds, Need Snakes, *from which this story is excerpted. His short fiction and poetry have appeared in such literary publications as* Proximity, Windmill, *and* Bombay Gin. *He helped launch a short-lived guerrilla zine, and his short story "Two Fingers Down" was nominated by the Veterans Writing Project for a 2017 Pushcart prize. He lives in Colorado with his wife, two cats, and two dogs.*

How Could You Do That?

By Eric Chandler
First-Place Poetry, 2019

It's a Christmas party.
Everybody is pretty lubed up.

I just read your article, he says.
(Here we go.)
I probably shouldn't,
but I'm going to ask you a question:
How could you do that?

Well, the story was about how I
didn't
shoot women and children.

Yeah, yeah, yeah,
but how could you do that?

(The story included
that
but it wasn't the point.)

I said,
no sane person wants to do
that.
Law of Armed Conflict.
Enemy combatants.
Et cetera.

Too late,
I know what I'd say now:
I have a question for you.
If you didn't like
that
maybe you should've done something about

that
other than asking me:
How could you do
(ew, gross)
that

Since you insist:
Because you sent me.
I was an extension of the will of the people.
You sent me.
The right bumper sticker on your car isn't enough.
You sent me.
You don't get to dismiss me by thanking me.
You sent me.
You don't get to forgive your own sins.
You sent me.
You are not absolved.
You sent me.
By commission or omission.
You sent me.
Last I checked, it was
We the People.

After you brush your teeth tomorrow,
put your face up to the mirror
and ask,

How could you do that?

Eric "Shmo" Chandler is a husband, father, and pilot who cross-country skis as fast as he can in Northern Minnesota. His poetry collection Hugging This Rock: Poems of Earth & Sky, Love & War *was published in 2017. He is also the author of a collection of outdoor essays called* Outside Duluth, *and a novella titled* Down In It. *His writing has appeared in* Northern Wilds, Grey Sparrow Journal, The Talking Stick, Flying Magazine, Sleet Magazine, O-Dark-Thirty, *and* Aqueous, *as well as others. He is a*

ERIC CHANDLER

member of Lake Superior Writers, the Outdoor Writers Association of America, and the Military Writers Guild. Chandler is also a veteran of both the U.S. Air Force and the Minnesota Air National Guard. He flew 145 combat missions and more than 3,000 hours in the F-16. He served in Iraq and Afghanistan. He enjoys cross-country ski racing and marathon running. He lives with his wife and two children in Duluth, Minnesota.

Good Soldier

By Sarah Maples
Second-Place Poetry, 2019

You have to call them sir

You have to call them sir
When they order you to drop
And give them twenty
When they tell the men
Not to be pussies
When they yell
Hey, female!

You have to call them sir

When they put you on duty
For the fifth weekend in a row
When they refuse
To look you in the eye
When they believe you can't do it
Because you're a woman

You have to call them sir

When they call you a disgrace
Because you have tits in uniform
When they snicker about how you're
A bitch, a slut, a dyke
When they say
No one is going to rescue
A fat girl from the battlefield

You have to call them sir

When they promise to be discreet
If you can ignore their wives
When they're drunk and
They say: don't tell
When you report it,
But they don't want to ruin his career

You have to call them sir

Only, you don't–
Have to call to them sir.

You only think you do.

Sarah Maples is a former U.S. Air Force intelligence officer and Afghan War veteran. She holds a Master of Fine Arts degree in Creative Writing from Fairleigh Dickinson University, and a graduate degree in publishing from George Washington University. Her writing has appeared in The Atlantic, Task & Purpose, Line of Advance, *and* Rally Point. *Maples is an associate editor for Military Experience & the Arts' literary journal* As You Were; *a freelance writer, editor, and writing coach; and founder of the veterans resource blog* After the DD-214.

Robert Olen Butler wants nachos

By Randy Brown
Third-Place Poetry, 2019

Author of 18 books
Pulitzer Prize-winner
Guggenheim fellow
Vietnam War veteran

tells the Air Force cadets
that Buddhists have it figured out:
We are all creatures of desire.

Last night at this time
I stood next to him in line at Hap's Lounge,
so I feel qualified to say at least this much:
At one point in his life
all Robert Olen Butler wanted
was some unbroken, circular tortilla chips.

Randy Brown embedded with his former Iowa Army National Guard unit as a civilian journalist in Afghanistan, May-June 2011. A 20-year veteran with one overseas deployment, he subsequently authored the 2015 poetry collection Welcome to FOB Haiku: War Poems from Inside the Wire. *His poetry and non-fiction have appeared widely in literary print and on-line publications. A member of the Military Writers Guild, he co-edited along with Steve Leonard the 2019 anthology* Why We Write: Craft Essays in Writing War. *He often blogs as "Charlie Sherpa."*

2020

Farragut Square

By Jillian Danback-McGhan
First-Place Prose (Veteran), 2020

Every day for the past year, I walked past the same man sitting on a park bench in Farragut Square rattling the meager change inside a Big Gulp cup. His pitch altered with the seasons:

"Help a man stay hy-drate-ed! Ain't no summer like those in the District!"

"It's cold again, folks! Freezing out here. Spare whatcha got before heading into those heated of-fi-ces!"

His bellowed appeals and resonant tenor echoed off both the historic, wrought iron and weathered stone buildings and the modern, glass and chrome edifices standing as sentinels around the Square. Most passers-by directed their eyes to some point far off in the distance. A few tossed dollar bills from their leather wallets before scurrying with their briefcases and totes into K Street offices. Even the statue of Admiral Farragut, the green, weathered bronze sculpture looming nearly 30 feet above the eponymous Square, seemed to divert his gaze at the squalor surrounding him.

Sometimes, the man brought cardboard signs. He had impeccable handwriting, a detail that belied his missing teeth and the layers of tattered rags he wore.

ITS RAININ' ITS POURIN'
CROWDSOURCE MY UMBRELLA

About a month later, he designed another sign, which immediately grabbed my attention:

GOT GUILT??
Donate Here!!

I gave him 20 dollars for that one. I can hardly escape my own sense of entitlement while living in this city. Besides, as a marketing professional, I had an appreciation for his craft.

"Well done," I told him as I handed him the folded bill.

"Glad you like it. Keep Freddie in mind next time!"

In the months that followed, I ensured I dropped few singles into his cup, or would purchase an extra coffee and a bagel for him every time I passed.

My meager daily offerings seemed pathetic against the sullen seasonal backdrop. The crisp charms of winter evade downtown Washington, D.C. in January. In its place is the harsh, foreboding chill of remembrance and soggy isolation. Gusts of cold wind funneled between buildings and gushed out in spontaneous, bitter torrents. The entire Square appeared gray and sodden, while the green statue of Admiral Farragut towered indifferently over the blots of faded fabric and weathered tents erected at the base of the statue. On the worst of one of these bleak mornings, one of Freddie's signs, propped at the marble base of Admiral Farragut's statue, once again caught my eye:

NAVY Man. Help me get
my anchor ~~away~~ aweigh

"Never knew you were in the Navy." I said, fishing out all the cash that I had in my wallet: 7 dollars. A gleeful smile spread across his chapped face. "I did my time in the Navy as well."

"Actually, this sign's a bit of a tall tale." Freddie responded. "I wasn't until just a short while ago, but now I'm working with the Admiral."

"Who?" I asked, glancing down at the empty liquor bottles and the American flag blanket peeking out of the garbage bag sitting at Freddie's feet.

Freddie pointed up. "Him," he said. "the Admiral." He lifted his hand, partially covered by the tattered remains of a filthy yellow glove, to the statue of Admiral Farragut.

"Ah," I said, and began to walk away. "I hope he doesn't keep you too busy."

"Thank you, dearest. He wanted me to let you know he sends his regards."

"Excuse me?" I abruptly stopped. A woman in a camel coat plowed into me as I turned to face him, diverting head-on into the steady stream of pedestrian traffic surging through the Square. Freddie merely pointed upwards again. "The Admiral says hello. Said you were the prettiest officer he ever seen."

My limbs stiffened. Freddie appeared in control of his faculties—surely, he didn't think he worked alongside a Civil War naval officer. Still, his comment awoke a dormant terror inside of me. I had walked through Farragut Square for almost a decade now, casually dismissing the link to my past it represented. That past now stood before me, a reminder from the most unlikely of messengers.

Realizing our conversation had delayed my arrival into the office, I wordlessly sprinted from Freddie and into my office building. I only had a moment to throw my bag upon my desk, shrug off my coat, and grab my notebook before heading into Peter's office for our 8 a.m. meeting.

Peter's office spanned the length of half of K Street and overlooked Farragut Square from four wide, floor-length windows. The morning sunlight filtered through the windows and glinted off of the silver picture frames and the crystal awards littering his desk. I squinted at the metallic haze it created as I stood in front of his open door.

"Vera!" Peter called and waved me in. My heels clicked noisily as I left the carpeted hallway and strode upon the hardwood floors that started at the threshold of his office.

"Grab a seat. Can Leah get you something? She's making me an espresso."

"I won't say no to coffee," I responded, sinking into the plush leather seat in front of his oak desk.

"Let's get down to it." He slapped his hands on his desktop, causing the smiling faces in the picture frames—turned outwards and precariously perched on the very edge of his desk—to leap upward in response.

"We haven't really had the chance to work together before. But I've heard great things about you. How long have you been one of our marketing directors?"

"Almost 10 years now," I replied. "After I left the Navy, I, um, took a year off, then went to graduate school, joined the firm shortly thereafter, and have been here ever since."

"Ah, that's right, a Navy girl," Peter replied. "What did you do?"

"I was on a ship, an officer. Spent about four years in, then decided it was time to do something different. I was on *USS Farragut*, actually, as luck would have it." I shook my head, attempting to chase away Freddie's words from this morning: *the Admiral says hello.* "Guess there's no escaping him."

Suddenly conscious of my trembling hands, I forced a quick laugh at the end of my sentence.

"Sorry?" Peter asked.

"Farragut was the name of the ship I was on when I was in the Navy. And Farragut Square is right across the street." I said, pointing out the window. "Funny coincidence, is all."

"Right." Peter replied. "I'm not one for city geography. Don't take the Metro, glide in and out of the parking garage under the building. But Farragut ... I read somewhere that the Navy has always had a ship by that name. Superstition or something."

"More tradition, really. The Navy's big on history, and he was the first Admiral. And, well," I watched Peter's eyes glaze over as I spoke. "Anyway, you mentioned you wanted to discuss a campaign with me?"

"Yes. This is the year you're looking to get promoted to partner, right?" Peter's attention quickly returned. He smiled when I nodded.

"Your promotion year is difficult, as you well know. You have to make the business case before the other partners, and it always helps to have a big-ticket account to your name. Which is why I called you in. But before we get into that, do you have a family?" He asked, motioning to the blonde figures smiling at me from within their silver frame.

"A family? Well, yes, my parents live outside of Philly. I try to take the train up and see them every month or so."

"No, not that. I meant kids? Husband?" Peter asked, then rapidly added, "Or wife. Partner-person."

I looked down again at the other pictures guarding the edge of Peter's desk: two girls and a boy who both appeared to be no more than ten, standing at the bottom of a ski lift; a slender woman with large diamond jewelry and wavy blonde hair sitting on the steps of a brick porch, holding a plump, drooling baby; a blonde, gangly boy with missing front teeth hugging a golden retriever.

"No. Nothing like that." I said, deliberately omitting the divorce I finalized six months ago.

"Well, then." Peter clapped his hands. "No one to miss you when I steal you away for the next three months. I'd like you to lead our newest campaign!"

I spent the rest of day staffing my team and building out our approach based upon the few client documents Peter sent my way. The new challenge served as a welcome distraction from the morning's events. Freddie's words and the uneasiness they stoked sunk into the recesses of my memory.

"Call your loved ones now so they don't report you missing!" Peter called as he passed by my office at 2:30 that afternoon, his briefcase and coat in hand.

Darkness shrouded the city when I departed the building at 7, stepping into the cruel slap of bitter wind funneling through the buildings lining both sides of the street. I traversed Farragut Square on my way to the Metro and noticed how the area transformed at night. An uneasy tension enveloped the area. Masses of blankets draped over and tucked around benches, creating make-shift tents on the street. Commuters held their bags more closely and intentionally avoided eye contact.

Streetlights cast amber light from above, causing pedestrians to drag long shadows on the sidewalk behind them. An umbra obscured Admiral Farragut's face, as if he closed his eyes in a dismissive slumber.

I saw Freddie leaning against the metro entrance, wrapped in layers of dirty towels and a sleeping bag with a broken zipper. A man in a dark coat and charcoal colored beanie hunched next to Freddie in conversation, his face wrapped a gray scarf. He darted away as I approached.

"There you are, dearest!" Freddie called. "Late one for you!"

"Yeah." I called back. That word: *dearest*. It had been so long since I heard it and felt the latent terror it elicited. That, along with the fierce cold, diminished any pathos welling in my chest that would have otherwise caused me to pull out my wallet.

"You'd better find someplace to get inside tonight. It's too cold out here for you."

Freddie smiled. "I was just talking to the Admiral, ya know. You just missed him. Said again how you were the prettiest officer he ever did see."

"Who told you to say that?" I asked, overwhelmed by a sudden flash of panic and the inexplicable sensation of sweating despite the cold. "Where are you getting this?" The current of Metro commuters flowed around us both at a distance.

"The Admiral, of course. He just left. He said he returned to check up on you." I shook my head. *You're overreacting. Freddie is drunk and telling wild stories and can tell he got a rise out of you. That's all.*

"Stop it. In fact, please stop talking to me." I told him in as dispassionate a voice as I could muster and darted into the gaping mouth of the metro entrance.

You're safe, I told myself, despite hyperventilating as soon as the metro doors closed. *You're safe.* I repeated this mantra the entire way home, attempting to calm my pounding heart and ease the dizziness. *You're being ridiculous.*

Back at home, I poured myself a glass of wine, then another, before calling Mary, my closest friend and former roommate when we both served together on Farragut. Our conversations and rare visits felt disjointed in the past few years, interrupted by the boisterous admonitions she directed toward one of her three children. Tonight, Mary managed to settle all her kids into bed for the evening and spoke without interruption. She congratulated me on the new campaign and updated me on her kids' latest attempts to fray her final nerve. When I told her about the incident with Freddie, her voice assumed a different tone.

"Let me get this straight—there's a homeless man living outside your office who is sending you messages from Admiral Farragut?" She asked. We both laughed, but I detected the concern in her voice.

"I know how it sounds. I'm not having a breakdown. Or, another, I guess. But something about it really creeped me out, Mary. Like I'm unable to escape the past. And I mean that literally: that fucking statue is right there and now I have some poor man running around saying things that remind me so much of … Does any of this make sense?"

"Look, I know you're not crazy," she replied. "But you have to trust yourself not to be, either. You had a hell of a time on that ship. I lived through it with you. And you've had your ups and downs since then. But it has been over ten years. It *is* in the past. And unlike my children, the past doesn't bite."

"No," I said, draining the contents of my wine and watching translucent, burgundy-tinted remnants of liquid bleed down the side of the glass in slow-moving rivulets. "But it can hurt like a bitch."

"Maybe you should talk to someone," she said softly.

"You know I have," I replied. "But it just keeps coming back, you know? Sometimes I'm relieved it does. That means I didn't make it all up. Like everyone thought I did."

I closed my eyes, weary from the day's excitement, and instantly heard a voice emerge from the recesses of my brain, male, authoritative, and sharp: *This is the type of accusation that can ruin a man's career. Are you sure you aren't overreacting?*

Could I ever be sure? I wondered.

"Look," Mary continued. "You have a stressful job, and with the divorce being so recent and all, I'm sure that brings up all kinds of old thoughts. But that's stuff's over now, Vera. Let it stay in the past."

That next morning, and for most mornings throughout the rest of January and February, I eschewed the Metro in favor of driving to work. I told myself it made more sense to drive. I left the office so late in the evening that it was probably safer that way. Shame piqued me in those rare moments I allowed myself to admit that I drove to avoid seeing Freddie in the Square.

The grueling pace of the campaign left little opportunity for self-reflection, though. I arrived at the office around 7:30, and never managed to leave until well after midnight. Peter seemed to vanish every time I needed him to weigh in on a decision, only to reappear with a vague criticism that required significant rework from our team. When I asked him about it, he merely shrugged and slapped me on the back: "You can figure it out. That's why we're going to make you a partner one day!"

Somewhere within the grueling haze of spending nearly all of my waking hours and weekends at the office, I managed to lose sight of the anxiety I felt about passing Freddie on the street. I still didn't take the Metro, but occasionally managed to work up enough courage to venture out onto K Street for coffee breaks.

During one such trip with Alex, one of my managers, I spotted Freddie. He had moved from the Square to the K Street sidewalk and transformed a bench into a cave of blankets and tarps from which only his eyes and nose were exposed. His eyes rolled back in a dreamlike state. A lanky, hunched, and hooded figure crouched beside him, nudging him gently. I almost passed by without Freddie noticing Alex and me.

Almost.

In a barely perceptible voice, I heard him call from beneath his ragged layers. His greeting caused my stomach to turn.

"Long time, dearest."

"Did you hear that?" I asked Alex.

"That homeless guy moaning?" She responded, flashing me a puzzled look.

"Never mind," I answered.

On our way back, we passed by Freddie again. He sat alone, his companion having apparently vanished. When he saw us, he grew animated and started to flair his arms. He lumbered from his hut and paced frantically and erratically in front of the bench.

"I have to tell you something, miss. It's real important." His voice slurred strangely, and he staggered as he approached us.

"Not now, Freddie. I need to go." I said, trying to act unperturbed.

"Do you know him?" Alex asked, quickly retreating away from where Freddie stood.

"I used to talk with him sometimes, but ..."

Freddie cut me off.

"It's the Admiral! Look, Miss, I don't know what he's about, but he's been asking for you and I don't like it. I didn't think nothing of it, and I'm sorry. I need to tell you." At that, he grabbed my right arm, causing me to jolt backwards and spill coffee down the sleeve of my jacket and stain his yellow-gloved hand.

Alex's eyes grew wide and she darted away into the safety of our office lobby only a few feet ahead of us.

"Let go!" I pulled my arm back and took off toward the building. Freddie followed.

"No, you don't understand. I did a bad thing. We need to talk to make this right."

I made it into the lobby just as two of our building security guards rushed out and grabbed Freddie by the arms. I paused to look back, watching Freddie struggle to push them away.

"Get inside," one guard yelled. "We'll come up for your statement later."

"Go easy," I said, feeling a stab of guilt in my chest as I looked back to watch them wrestle Freddie out of the lobby. "There's something wrong with him today. He ... He's different."

"Inside!" the other ordered.

About an hour later, the security guards met me in my office with a police officer following them. They asked me to relate the events of the morning as well as any other previous interactions I had with Freddie.

"Did something else happen?" I asked, realizing their line of interrogation exceeded the scope of today's encounter. The officer looked at the security guards then closed his notebook.

"Freddie, as you referred to him, is Mr. Frederick Williams. He had his ID on him. He apparently stays with his sister most days, but heads out into the streets from time to time when she kicks him out because of his drinking. Some mental issues, nothing violent apparently, but causes him to reject any kind of help. Today, it looks like he overdosed. He started seizing after he grabbed you earlier and we sent him to National in an ambulance."

"Overdose?" I asked. "I've seen him drunk, yes, but he's never been high, that I could tell at least. I've been chatting with him in passing for a little over a year. He's clever. Charming at times."

"They all have a trigger." the police officer responded. "The cold sometimes does it. Causes people to get desperate. What's strange is that he had a large quantity of money on him, which means he might have stolen that along with the drugs. Again, desperation. Doubt we'll ever find out. Thefts like that don't get reported." The officer and the two guards stood. I accepted the officer's card and escorted them to the elevators.

Freddie never seemed like the type of person who would steal, I thought. He seemed docile. Even in his drug-addled state, he seemed more worried than angry. I started to hyperventilate as I thought of him sitting in the emergency room on his own, and went over our earlier interaction again and again. *Are you sure you're not overreacting?*

Later that evening, I called the hospital to check up on his status, but staff wouldn't reveal any of his information since I wasn't a family member.

Did I want him to recover? I wondered, hating myself for the momentary sense of relief that lapped over me. Regardless, I ventured out of the office for more frequent breaks, peering into every blanketed mound to see if Freddie had returned. I never saw him again.

By early March, a cold but humid fog descended over the city, making the sidewalks slick with condensation. Walking outside felt like putting on a still-wet bathing suit before venturing to the pool. A light blue haze hung over the Square when I commuted into work in the mornings, and daylight stretched its cramped limbs further and further into the evening as if to cautiously test out the boundaries of how far it could go. Although most days were still wet and bitter, portents of spring appeared subtly and in unexpected ways: salt strips abating from the roads, rain flowing from sidewalk cracks and into sewer drains like tiny streams, enthusiastic chirps from the robins gathering in alleyways.

Hope no longer felt foolish.

Around this time, the marketing campaign wrapped up. Our team held a small celebration in the office, jovially sipping slightly acidic wine from clear plastic cups, while Peter attended the official launch party with the client. The team scattered around 8 p.m. I retreated to my office to respond to a few e-mails long neglected due to the final surges of the campaign launch. The time on my laptop read 11:19 when I finally looked up from my work. Habituated to the loneliness, eerie groanings, and absurd silence of the office after hours, somehow three hours evaporated in front of my keyboard.

I packed up my work bag and shut my office door, watching the motion-sensing lights snap on as I continued down the empty corridor and to the elevator lobby. The void felt familiar and strangely comforting now. I braved the solitude alone, brazenly and triumphantly stepping into the elevator that carried me down into the parking garage underneath the building.

My victorious deportment proved to be short lived. When I reached my car, I glanced up at the parking tag tucked into the driver's side visor, noticing my monthly parking pass had expired. I would have to pay at the parking kiosk before exiting the garage.

The parking kiosk resided in a long rectangular vestibule, surrounded on three sides by glass, with a single glass door providing the only entrance or exit to the space. I left my car idling directly in front of the door, and jumped out with my credit card in hand. Inside the vestibule, a robotic voice emanated from the kiosk, repeating "Please insert your parking ticket" with the urgency of a fire alarm.

As I waited for the machine to spit out my card, I heard a creak and caught the door swing open from the corner of my left eye. I started, unaware of anyone else remaining in the building, let alone the garage.

"Hello, dearest," he said.

I froze, enveloped by panic.

That voice. I identified it long before I turned to examine the figure before me. Wiry and tall, slightly stooped. I peered into his face, trying to reconcile it with the features I once knew: hollow cheekbones and a prominent jaw, both covered by dark stubbled flecked with white. He wore a charcoal gray beanie, pulled low over his forehead and partially obscuring his deeply set eyes.

Could that really be him? I wondered. I doubted my memories for far too long to rely on them.

But his voice. That I would remember until my dying day.

"Terry?" I asked. "Terry, is that you?" I stammered again.

He slowly nodded his head.

"What are you doing here?" He stood there, silent, smiling the twisted smile that for years prevented me from closing my eyes at night.

"What are you doing here?" I repeated. "You know you're not supposed to be anywhere near me."

"Didn't you get my messages?" He asked.

"What messages?" I asked. "You know you're not supposed to contact me."

"The ones from Freddie, of course. He was so eager. A bit slow, though," Terry said. "Don't you know, I told him I was Admiral Farragut when we first met. Thought you'd pick up on the reference. The poor drunken fool, I think he believed me. That, or I paid him too well for him to even bother asking."

"You ... *you* were the one telling him to say those things." The hooded figure next to Freddie. Of course.

Every incident I attempted to repress from the past decade streamed through my head with immense, glaring clarity and violently collided into the reality I constructed in my current life: the cryptic messages Terry would write on my car window; the notes I'd find in my purse when I thought I was out alone, in my kitchen when I thought the apartment was empty. When I awoke in my stateroom on the ship in the middle of the night to find him standing over my bed.

You are the prettiest officer I've ever seen, his first note read. I was 24 at the time, and stupidly thought of a note from a much-older officer as a harmless flirtation.

Don't you dare fucking play with me. I will find you, read the last note, the one that appeared on my windshield when I was visiting a friend in another state.

You tried so hard to forget, I thought, a*nd look what happened.*

I started to hyperventilate, though it felt remote and surreal, as if my chest existed separately from my body and someone else's breaths were forced in and out of my lungs.

"Didn't you like them, dearest?" Terry asked. "It's been far too long since I sent you a message. I wanted to make an effort."

"Don't come any closer. There are cameras all over this building." I cringed listening to my quivering voice. *There were cameras, weren't they? The car is right there. If I could only get past him.*

"Those cameras?" Terry gestured up toward a small white cylinder bolted to the ceiling above his head and roughly half a stride in front of him. I shifted my eyes up in a sequence of short glances, too terrified to look away from Terry for longer than the duration of a single one of my frantic heartbeats. The camera pointed away from the door and toward the payment kiosk. From that angle, it captured my every motion while Terry remained behind the lens, completely out of view.

He always knew how far to go, I thought. *They'll only see me: a frantic woman reacting to something invisible.*

"They won't see me, dearest. Which means no one will believe you." He hissed. "Just like last time. Everyone thought you made it all up, you know. Remember all the things they said about you afterward?" He clucked his tongue in mock censure.

"I know what they said, but they believed me enough to give me a restraining order against you."

"A military protective order, dearest. That's long expired now. Sure, they forced me to retire early. But they also sent you to that hospital so you wouldn't try to hurt yourself again." He let out a short, mirthless laugh. "I think I got the better deal."

I frantically glanced side to side. The expansive bottom floor of the parking garage, completely deserted for the evening, stretched out on all sides, promising escape. But the glass walls boxed me in on all sides.

"You need to leave." I said.

Terry merely stood and stared back, solemnly shaking his head. My card remained half consumed by the machine, causing it to release high-pitched pleas for attention that reverberated, unnoticed, throughout the tiny space.

"You really should've listened to Freddie, you know. He practically told you I was here, but you ignored him. You'd think you'd be more sympathetic."

Freddie, I thought mournfully, fighting a wave of nausea rising from my stomach. "What did you do to him? He did what you wanted, why would you hurt him?"

"Think he figured something was up in one of his sober moments. Went back on the deal we had. Said he was done passing along messages and updating me on your whereabouts. So I had to show him there were consequences for betraying me." Terry's face changed sharply. He bared his teeth and squinted his eyes into a vicious expression. "You both needed to be taught."

I stepped backwards cautiously, certain he'd spring forward at any moment, until I collided with the glass wall at the farthest corner of the vestibule. Terry remained impassive.

"Jesus Christ, Terry." The words left my throat like the garbled end of an echo. "It's been over 10 years! Move on, for God's sake! Are you for real with this?"

"Oh dearest, I think the better question is if I'm real at all," he said. "People thought you were crazy, you know. Still do. Just another hysterical woman who couldn't take the pressure of being in the military. The better question is ... do *you* believe I'm really here? Or are you imagining things again?"

I involuntarily traced the inside of my wrist, feeling the raised bumps running down my forearm, barely palpable through the thin silk fabric. They had almost faded. Almost.

"Not for a moment. You're the one who's delusional. Always have been."

"Then come over here and see for yourself." Terry crossed his arms. "Touch me and see if I'm real. Or see if you're just going crazy again. It's a stressful time for you, dearest. I heard that triggers some strong emotions." He stood still and stared back at me, daring me to move.

I willed myself to stride toward him with arms outstretched, proving to him I that wasn't afraid. That he couldn't control me any longer. Instead, my hands clawed against the cold glass behind me.

"Just as I thought. You can't be bothered, just like the old times. Here I am, trying so hard to get your attention, but you still think you're too good for the likes of me. Just like before when you flung yourself in front of me and tossed me away."

"I never did!" I shrieked and stepped forward with a fury that momentarily caused my fear to dissipate and paralyzed all sense of reason. "Never, not for a moment. I know exactly what happened!"

"Don't you fucking dare tell me what happened." He bellowed.

I recoiled in response to his outburst and crumbled to the floor more violently than if I had been struck. Terry laughed at my response.

"I am the one who was wronged, made to look like a fucking idiot! You led me on, thinking the entire time that you were too good for me, too smart, that I was just to be fooled with. And you thought you'd get away by telling all sorts of lies about me, making the Navy put up an invisible fence to make me disappear."

He paused and flashed a cold, triumphant smile. "No. It doesn't work like that. You had to pay for that fence with your reputation. I warned you that you would. But that's not enough. Now you get to know how it feels to always be thinking of someone."

As he finished his sentence, he lurched forward, springing like a snake ready to strike. I shrieked and threw my arms over my head, as if to shield myself, shaking and sobbing uncontrollably, startling myself with the repellent, putrid sounds that emerged from my mouth.

"Don't worry," he continued, his face sanguine in response to my crumbled condition. "I'm not going to hurt you, dearest—not now, at least. But I'll be wherever you are. Watching as you get your groceries with those cute little yellow bags, or when you head to Penn Station for monthly treks to see your folks. Just like I did the night Scott stormed out of your old townhouse and went to that bar down the street. I actually sent him a beer from across the bar, you know. Poor bastard. I knew just how he was feeling."

That was the night I told Scott I wanted a divorce, I remembered. The night I told him I married him to feel secure without realizing I never actually would. That he couldn't help me. That I couldn't trust him or anyone else. Scott said I needed to get over it, the past belonged in the past. The past bought him a drink that night.

"Maybe one day I'll get impatient, like that time outside of your apartment when I had to smash your windshield to get your attention. I hate it when you make me do dramatic things like that. Maybe I'll have to punish you like poor Freddie. Or I might just get bored and leave you alone. But this much I do know. We belong together. And I'll always be with you. In person," he held out his hands to emphasize his point and slowly backed away to the door. "Or in your mind."

With that, he walked backwards out of the vestibule, grinning at me the entire time, and disappeared around a corner.

I don't remember anything after that. Overwhelmed by emotion, I must have plunged into some overstimulated fugue state, which caused me to black out.

When I came to, I found myself in the driver's seat of my idling car, unsure of how much time had elapsed. Dazed and shaking, I slowly regained my awareness and noticed the alarms violently chiming throughout the vehicle. Blurry forms and shadows gradually coalesced into discernible landmarks. The soft glow of amber streetlights illuminated the scene in front of me. I had turned the wrong way into I Street, veered past the bus lane, drove onto the curb, and crashed into a stone marker lining the boundaries of Farragut Square. My windshield wipers dragged loudly and wildly across the glass even though it wasn't raining. I looked down and traced a trail of crusted vomit on the front of my dress with a trembling hand.

Directly ahead stood Admiral Farragut, illuminated by a series of upward pointing, faintly flickering bulbs. His head tilted to the left, casting his apathetic, verdigris-crusted gaze into the distance, willfully overlooking the commotion below.

Jillian Danback-McGhan is a U.S. Navy veteran. Her writing appears or is forthcoming in such venues as Minerva Rising, Prometheus Dreaming, *and the anthology* A Common Bond, Vol. 3. *By day, Danback-McGhan works as a management consultant and executive coach; by night (and all the cracks of time in-between), she works on her collection of short fiction. She is a graduate of Georgetown University, George Mason University, and the U.S Naval Academy. She lives in Annapolis, Maryland with her family.*

Leroy's Blues

By Terry Sanville
Second-Place Prose (Veteran), 2020

They don't build ships like those anymore. These days, cargo vessels are floating bricks, huge container craft a couple of blocks long. But, in 1969, freighters that could haul maybe 7,000 tons steamed upriver to Newport, a supply terminal a few klicks outside of Saigon. I worked there as a stevedore in the U.S. Army during the Vietnam War. Can't say for sure how this college guy ended up on the docks unloading 4-hold freighters in the blistering sun. Bad luck I guess. More likely, it was my bad attitude.

I lived on Long Binh Army Base, in a corrugated metal hooch with 20 other G.I.s, part of a company of nearly three hundred truck drivers and stevedores. I'd been assigned to the office, to prepare Morning Reports and other paperwork. But I mouthed off to a sergeant and disobeyed an order, got busted back to Private, then assigned to a ship platoon. I knew nothing about ships or unloading them. But then, neither did Leroy.

Big, black and from the Watts neighborhood of LA, Leroy kept to himself, read *Ebony* magazine, and listened to soul music on his tiny record player. Being white bread from Santa Barbara, I had little in common with him, except for music. At night I'd haul my guitar outside onto the raised boardwalk that connected all the hooches, and clumsily play '60s protest songs, folk music, and a little rock.

"Where'd ya learn ta play?" Leroy asked one night.

"Ah, ya know, just picked it up."

He stood over me, his hulking body blocking the glare from the descending flares blazing in the black sky above the base perimeter.

"Ever play blues?" he asked.

I grinned. "Nah, too many notes."

"Just play the right ones."

"Can you play?"

He nodded.

"How can you stand being without a guitar?"

"I can't."

Leroy slumped onto the boardwalk next to me and leaned back

against the hooch's metal wall. I passed him my ax. He used his big thumb and fat fingers on his right hand to pluck the strings while bending them with his left-hand fingers. Blues sounds poured from my little Harmony.

"That's damn good," I said.

"Feels good."

"Yeah."

After work and chow, we'd meet on the boardwalk. Sometimes we'd smuggle a couple of beers out of the EM Club to prime the pump. I'd let Leroy play for an hour or so, then beg him to show me some of his moves, strange chord fragments and notes flying past. He'd hum along as he played.

"Why don' ya sing something?" I asked.

"Don' like ma voice. But the damn sound jus' comes out. Can't stop it."

"Yeah."

The rest of the guys pretty much left us alone. But a few joked that a white boy didn't have the soul to play Black music. As the months passed, I caught glimpses of where that music came from as Leroy's life story slowly leaked out, mostly a cliché by today's standards but strange to me, a 20-year-old Catholic kid that never knew poverty, abuse, or overt racism before shipping out to Vietnam. But Leroy had his own unique wrinkles: quitting high school after the Watts riots in '65 burned down his family's grocery; living next to the LA River in a hobo camp; hitchhiking to San Francisco to check out Haight-Ashbury. With no skills or student deferment, he got drafted and landed on the same docks as me. The Army was good at throwing people together that normally would never meet.

Every morning in the dark, we stevedores boarded deuce-and-a-halfs and rumbled south along Charlie Road to Newport. We worked 12-hour shifts. Of all the jobs, Leroy had one of the better ones. He operated a winch that lifted cargo out of a freighter's hold and placed it on the dock, to be whisked away to storage sheds by huge forklifts. While *he* sat on his deck seat in the afternoon breeze, operating the winch, us shirtless stevedores struggled to hook steel cables to pallets of cargo, down in the breathless holds where temperatures topped 110.

At lunch, Leroy and I hung out behind a metal storage container and smoked a joint bought from one of the dockside mama-sans. He talked about blues and soul music, one of his favorites being *Dock of the Bay* by Otis Redding–a good song for stevedores, *"Watchin' the ships roll in ..."*

"Yeah, it's kinda pop ... but sad, too," Leroy told me.

"Can you play it?"

"No sweat, man. I'll show ya."

It became my favorite tune, an anthem to my year spent in 'Nam. When I play it now, it takes me back to Newport and those hustling docks where a bunch of yahoos from all over the states unloaded ships and dreamed about going home.

Vietnam's hot-and-dry season hit hard. The wind off the mocha-colored Saigon River brought the smell of poverty and desperation. We had survived another Tet Offensive by the Viet Cong. Freighters from all over the world crowded Newport and the river, waiting to be unloaded. The officers pushed us, the sergeants yelled at us to pick up the pace, with a record for tonnage unloaded being the supposed prize for us low-level stevedores.

Late one afternoon, we'd almost finished with the bottom level of the front hold on a Canadian freighter. Sweat soaked the bandana tied around my head and dripped into my eyes. The steel cables had sliced and diced my bare arms. My lips had cracked. We took a break in the meager shade against the freighter's hull, breathing hard, pouring warm water over our heads and swearing.

Sergeant Lopez stared down at us from topside. "Hey, no breaks until ya finish. Now move it."

With grumbled curses, our 6-man crew stood and prepared to resume the unloading.

"Fuck 'im," Johnson muttered.

McPherson snorted. "Yeah, that mother-fucker's probably in the fuckin' office already, feet up, bullshittin' with the rest of the fuckin' lifers."

As the hours passed and the heat rose, our use of the F-bomb increased. "Let's jus' finish it," I said.

McPherson climbed onto the seat of his tiny forklift. He used it to move the pallets of cargo from the outer edges of the hold into its center. Once properly positioned, we slid the cables under each pallet and attached their loop ends to the hook that Leroy had dropped down to us. Once secured, Leroy hauled the cargo skyward. We worked hard until there were just two crates left.

McPherson raised the machine's forks to about 2 feet off the plates and stomped on the gas. The forklift shot forward and speared a 5-foot-tall cardboard crate. He backed up. Foam sprayed from the square holes. We stared open-mouthed at the damage he'd done.

McPherson jumped down and took a whiff, then dipped a finger into the puddle forming at his feet and stuck it in his mouth. A shit-eating grin spread across his face.

"Hey guys, it's beer."

With a shout, the rest of us charged forward and tore into the crate, pulling back the cardboard to expose cans of Pabst Blue Ribbon. Brody produced a bayonet and began stabbing holes in their tops. We greedily sucked out the hot beer, flung the empties into the shadows, and laughed our asses off.

Johnson broke into the crate next to the beer that had Hormel Company labeling. We found a shitload of canned meat. We each grabbed an armful of beers and retreated into the shade to guzzle hot suds and chow down baked ham.

In a little while, Leroy descended the 40-foot ladder from topside and joined us.

"Where ya been, cool breeze?" I asked and jabbed him in the ribs.

"Been keepin' an eye out for Lopez. Ya know he'll come back to check on you fools."

"Yeah, so?" Brody said. "What cun they do? We're already in hell."

Leroy grinned. I handed him a beer and he downed it with one quick tilt of the can.

With the temperature well over 100, most of the guys got drunk after only a couple-three beers. The gang quieted, heads drooped against sweat-covered chests.

"Come on," Leroy said, "we gotta hurry." He began grabbing guys and walking them to the ladder to climb out of the hold. Most could only manage a single rung before falling back, too drunk to make it.

Leroy scrambled topside and yelled down, "Heads up."

The winch's hook dropped toward us, an old fashioned cargo net attached. When it hit bottom, Leroy came down and spread the net across the plates.

"Get in and sit down," he commanded.

We shambled out of the shadows and sat on the net while Leroy looped its corners onto the winch hook. Again, he scrambled up the ladder. Watching him made me sweat even more. In a flash, we soared upward, rising from the depths of Hades toward heaven in a tangle of arms and legs. We clung to the netting as Leroy swung us out over portside and lowered us to the concrete dock below. We landed gently.

I guess I was the most sober because I managed to unhook the net and we hauled-ass out of that thing and staggered toward the trucks parked at the edge of the terminal. In the background I heard Sgt. Lopez screaming, "Get back here, you assholes. That's an order." But none of us stopped.

That night, Lopez told us that we'd all get Article 15s–a mild court martial of sorts–for disobeying a direct order and destroying government property. But the Army couldn't afford to slow its freight.

The next morning, with pounding heads, we rumbled down Charlie Road to unload more ships and bake in the oven-hot holds. And our first sergeant and commanding officer hated all the paperwork that Article 15s required and let us slide. Turns out, they weren't total assholes after all.

A week later poor Leroy got into trouble. He was working the winch, lifting a 4-ton crate out of the hold and had swung it over the ship's side when, for some reason, he jerked the controls. The cargo abruptly stopped in mid-lift, at least 50 foot up. A cable dislodged and the damn thing tumbled end-over-end to the dock below. The wooden crate exploded and scattered its contents, pieces flying everywhere. It contained air conditioners, most likely headed to some officers' club or maybe an Army headquarters building. The Lifers would be pissed.

In a month, Leroy got shipped out to a trucking unit up north near the DMZ. As far as I knew, he'd never driven big trucks before – but then he'd never operated a freighter's winch before either.

On his last night, we smoked a joint in the abandoned rubber tree grove, on the hill in back of our company area. The perimeter lit up with flares but otherwise stayed quiet.

"So how short are ya?" Leroy asked.

"I got two weeks 'til DEROS."

"Shit man, I got four months before I get on that Freedom Bird."

"You'll do OK, just keep the trucks outta the ditch."

He grinned. "Yeah, ya know, back in the world I don' even have a driver's license."

"It wouldn't help over here. You see the way everyone drives."

From our hillside position we could see the base's perimeter fencing, the guards in their towers, the row-on-row of concertina wire, the ground studded with Claymore mines, the bunkers with machine gun ports. I began to play the Harmony, showing off the blues riffs I'd learned from Leroy. We passed the guitar back and forth for a couple hours. Finally we got up to leave.

I handed Leroy the Harmony. "Here, take her with you."

He stared at me wide-eyed. "Nah, man, it's ... it's too much."

"Don't sweat it. I'll be home soon, got another ax there to play."

"Thanks, man."

"But you gotta leave the guitar behind when you go back to the world. Give it to somebody learnin' to play. Make sure they promise to pass it on."

Leroy survived the war. But what he did or where he went remains a mystery to me. These days, when I play guitar I sometimes think about the Harmony, maybe hanging on some wall in downtown Hue, beat to hell, still leaking notes, but only the right ones.

Terry Sanville lives in San Luis Obispo, California with his artist-poet wife (his in-house editor) and two plump cats (his in-house critics). More than 400 of his stories and essays have appeared in venues such as The Potomac Review, The Bryant Literary Review, *and* Shenandoah. *He was nominated twice for Pushcart Prizes, and once for Best of the Net. Branching Realities released his debut novel,* Face-to-Face. *Sanville is a retired urban planner and an accomplished jazz and blues guitarist. He once played with a symphony orchestra backing up jazz legend George Shearing.*

Library in White Cedar

By Edward Ahern

Third-Place Prose (Veteran), 2020

The two-day drive from Connecticut to White Cedar, Michigan was endless neon chain links- the same motels, gas stations, and restaurants sprouting up about every ten miles along the interstate.

I was on my way to assist at the funeral of the library in White Cedar. My great, great grandfather, Thomas Willman, had provided the money to build the library and on his death had bequeathed his books to it. He'd specified that if the town closed the library the books should be returned to his heirs. I was the only surviving descendent the town had found, and I'd rented a large SUV in case the books were worth claiming.

Cathy Bender, the town librarian, had been the one to call. Her voice had that slight midwestern nasality that some easterners find annoying but I had always liked.

"Mr. Willman, praise the Lord I was able to find you. We need to talk about the Willman books in our library."

"Call me John, please. What about them?"

"White Cedar can't support the library any more, and has to close it."

"Maybe get some cultural aid money from the state."

"Ah. Well, they're radical Democrats and we're solid Tea Party, so they don't look too kindly on us."

I paused. "Well, Cathy, I could be classified as one of those rad libs."

There was a pause on her end. "Well, you seem nice anyway, John, we just won't talk politics."

Or religion, I thought.

Cathy and I spent the next 15 minutes talking safely if boringly about White Cedar and its recent activities. Her voice had a pleasing brook burble to it, and I let her flow.

I drove into town the late afternoon of the second day. The main street had only one traffic light—a flashing yellow. Many of the storefronts were papered over, and those still clear-glassed looked grimy. White Cedar was dying, one organ at a time, and it was the library's turn. There were no pedestrians, and the only hint of congestion was at the gas-station-*cum*-convenience-store. Beer sales apparently were still good. I parked in the overgrown lot of an abandoned Kmart and called Cathy.

"Cathy? It's John Willman. I just got into town."

"Depressing isn't it, John. The nearest motel is about 7 miles down the state road, in case you've changed your mind about staying with me. It's not Marriott, but it's comfortable, and I could use the money. I have Wi-Fi."

After two days of blurring Motel Six, Days Inn and Red Roof signs, I wanted local. "Still 40 dollars a day?"

"Yes. Is that too much?"

"It's fine. I'm guessing meals aren't included?"

"No, but the diner down the street is open early-to-late and could use the business, too."

It took a full three minutes to drive to her house. She was waiting on the front porch. "We've talked so much on the phone, John, I feel like I know you."

Cathy was petite, slim and short-haired. We said hello again and hugged because it seemed the thing to do. She felt nice. We walked my bags up to an upstairs bedroom and came back down into a front room stuffed with old furniture. She called it a parlor. "I can do credit cards, but if you pay me by cash or check it saves me money."

My checkbook was 750 miles away. "Ah, no problem, I'll just hit an ATM when I go for dinner."

I looked at Cathy more closely. She'd graduated from 40, but then so had I. Her expression had a weathered, inquisitive quality, as if despite bad treatment she was still open to experience. "Look, if you haven't eaten, would you mind coming with me to dinner? You could fill me in on the library and what we need to do. My treat."

She didn't bother to protest, which I liked. "Sure. I haven't eaten there in weeks."

The diner had a faint background aroma of rancid grease. Cathy said first-name hellos to the other eaters and the waitress and introduced me, although I assumed that they already knew who I was and why I was there.

She didn't drink alcohol, so neither did I. After we'd coated our stomachs with fried food, we started talking about the library's last rites. "Once the elementary school closed and the kids started getting bussed to Smithdale, the library emptied out. There's no money to fix the building or buy books, hasn't been for years. My title is librarian, but I'm just an unpaid caretaker.

"A book merchant will take all the other titles, John, but at 30 cents apiece. We'll get four-thousand dollars, which will barely cover closing up the building and paying off the utility bills. Except of course for your great, great grandfather's collection. That's in a separate room. Doris Lunning, the last real librarian, limited access to the collection to what she called 'serious scholars.' Nobody claims to be that in White Cedar, so the collection just got dusty."

I was familiar with dead ends-the childless remnant of the Willman line, with family records and photos mailed to me as other relatives had passed on. Records that included a listing of the books in the Willman collection. I'd emailed the descriptions to two dealers for initial appraisals.

Cathy wore what looked to be an engagement ring on a right-hand finger. She caught my glance and puckered her mouth. "It's what you're guessing. Six years of un-bliss and a divorce. He was a jerk and I kept the ring. He left town."

"Kids?"

"No, thank the Lord. Although I wanted them."

"Same story, different perspective. She left me for another guy, but did give the ring back. Keep it in my hope chest."

Cathy laughed. The resonance was pleasant. Then her expression tightened into serious.

"I've talked with the mayor about the Willman books. They were, after all, willed to the town. Wouldn't it be the right thing us to find another home for them? You could just sign a waiver giving the books to us."

I wondered. If they were trying to get legal rights to those antique books there might be something more to them than paper lice.

"Sell them off, you mean."

"Yes, but as a collection that would be housed in another library, and would live on as a collection under the Willman name. You've seen what our town has become, we're in desperate need of funds. It would be beneficial for both you and us."

I studied the four wilted French Fries left on my plate. "Interesting possibility, Cathy, but before I decide on anything, I need to know what the books are worth. It'll take a few days to hear back, and meanwhile I need to go through the library and verify their condition."

She touched my hand. "That sounds like a polite 'no.' Please don't slam the door on us, John–leave it ajar, while we keep talking."

I realized I didn't want to go back to suitcases and WiFi. "Is there any place left in town where you can watch me drink?"

She laughed again. "We haven't sunk quite that far. There are two bars, one for the beer-and-shot crowd, and one with cocktail napkins under the glasses."

"Upscale, please."

We could have walked to the bar, but I drove. Cathy also knew all five people there, and introduced me as 'the Willman heir.' I cringed, because it made me sound like someone ripe for donating.

She ordered cola, I ordered scotch-and-soda. We avoided discussing the library, and peeked into each other's lives. I knew she was a born again Christian and staunch conservative, which took several other topics out of play.

Cathy described losing her last job when the local car dealership closed, and having no immediate prospects for a new one. I downplayed my position in an academic think tank, but she called me out.

"Don't give me that false modesty. I looked you up. You're a senior fellow. And a successful politician before that." She said it with a forgiving grin and I shrugged admittance. Our chatter quick-stepped from topic to topic, and I reluctantly called it a night after two drinks. I didn't want the one cop on night shift to bust me for DWI.

On the drive back, she offered to provide breakfast before we went over to the library, and I immediately accepted. Back at her house, we settled into saggy cushioned easy chairs in the living room. She kept surprising me. She'd gone to college on a scholarship, and used her teaching degree to get a job at the town elementary school. A job that disappeared when the school closed. The well-used house we sat in had been her parents and grandparents. Cathy was attached and beholden to a town that would, like her husband, leave her. When we stood up, I wanted to kiss her cheek, but just shook hands before I went upstairs.

Once in bed, lights off, I realized it was too dark and too quiet. I missed my overdeveloped suburb and its white-noise pacifier.

I smirked after coming downstairs the next morning. We were both dressed in flannel shirts and jeans, ready for dusty work. Breakfast was healthy—yogurt, juice and wheat toast—and I guessed that Cathy had eaten her chicken-fried steak the night before as a gesture for me.

The library building, a small Victorian, sagged both outside and in, and water stains blotched the paper on several walls. The building was uninsurable and probably uninhabitable. I raised an eyebrow at Cathy and she shrugged. "I warned you we were on hard times."

The Willman collection was in an interior room, musty but dry. It needed to be moved soon, before the cloth covered electrical wiring or a water leak attacked. But even dusty and unused it was impressive: 350 books, about half of them leather-bound, with several outsized folios. According to my list, the last book had been added in 1902.

I'd brought my laptop, and I held it up. "Do we have service?"

"We pirate Internet from the auto-supply store next door. They know about it, of course."

Small towns are without secrets, and I assumed last night's house sharing was already under discussion. I'd started taking cell phone photos and sending them off to the book appraisers, when an overdue thought struck me.

"Cathy, I'm guessing you've already had the collection evaluated?"

She paused. "Sort of. We couldn't afford a real appraisal, but sent a list to the book dealer in Grand Rapids who's buying all the other books."

"What did he offer for the Willman lot?"

There was a longer pause. "Twenty-three thousand. We have no idea if that's fair."

"Neither do I. But I will. The two companies I'm using won't be bidding on the lot, so they'll hopefully be honest."

Cathy left me alone in the Willman room and went over to the desk top computer at the checkout desk. After I'd sent off pictures and details, I started browsing through the records, trying to get a feel for who my great, great grandfather had been. His obituary was fulsome with praise, but family gossip had told of a cunning and ruthless businessman. I wondered if the library building and the impressive books had been his repayment to all the townspeople he'd skinned.

As I was gingerly leafing through the books, I got an e-mail back from Dulters and Wilkins, one of the appraisers:

Advisory on the Thomas McKinney History of the Indian Tribes of

North America, three volumes 1838, 1842 and 1844, inscribed by McKinney to Henry Clay and containing pasted-in Ex Libris bookplates of Henry Clay, signed by him. Impossible to provide formal valuation without physical examination, but initial indication unsigned is $170,000 and signed by author and Henry Clay $225,000. Other valuations to follow.

I stared at nothing. The book dealer Cathy had mentioned would have at least a vague idea of the value of the McKinney books, which meant either he was playing the town of White Cedar or Cathy was playing me.

She'd left me alone in the Willman room and after another hour I realized I wanted her company and walked over to the main desk. She was watching videos on her cell phone. In the three hours we'd been there not another person had entered.

"Lonely work."

"And I usually shirk it. I stay home, and just leave a sign on the entry door that anyone who wants to use the library should call me so I could open it up. No one does."

I wondered if it wasn't equally boring at home, but said nothing. I lifted the countertop hatch, went into librarian territory, and sat at a desk facing Cathy's. "You should get out of here."

"And go home?"

"No, move out, find a town with a pulse, and get the teaching job you deserve."

She showed me that smile again. "And leave all this? I get by, sort of, on alimony and some left over money. Nobody would buy the house, so I'd just have to board it up and abandon it. Except for college, everything I know and am is here, including my church. Moving away would be like abandoning a sick relative I should be caring for. Does that sound stupid?"

"A little. But I've never had the relationship with place like you're talking about. Look, let's get out of Sleepy Hollow this evening. Bentonville is less than an hour away, and, according to my laptop, has six restaurants and a multiplex theater. Could I entice you into a movie and dinner?"

"Well aren't you suave. Of course. A woman my age shouldn't turn down a date."

Once we'd locked up the library, we stopped back at Cathy's house to change before heading out. The speed-limit-plus-ten conversation was haphazard, because our frames of reference not only didn't overlap, they almost didn't abut. Her temperament suited me, but I was a fervently liberal atheist intrigued with a born-again Tea Partier. Despite that, we laughed a lot.

After we'd left the restaurant, I turned to her in my car.

"Cathy, I need to tell you up-front that I'm going to keep the Willman books. I feel about the books the way you feel about White Cedar. I want to shepherd them for one more generation. I'll be leaving in a couple days and will pack them up and take them with me."

I studied her while I said this. She looked relieved rather than disappointed. "I had to ask about them, but that's fine, they're your books, after all."

"It's great that you understand. I need to make a quick stop at the pharmacy before we head back."

The ride back was quieter, the conversation more piquant. We'd only met the day before, and my departure was already in sight. Once back in her house we sat close together on the living room couch.

We kissed, lightly, and then again more seriously. Without words we began to gently explore each other, the geriatric sofa complaining about our shifts in position.

Cathy leaned back slightly and looked at me. "Does your pit stop at the out of town drugstore mean what I think it does?"

"Afraid so."

"I appreciate your discretion." She smiled, and we resumed, two long-abstinent adults relying on muscle memory. Once we subsided and snuggled together, the sofa got its revenge, and my twisted back began to cramp. Eventually I gave up and suggested she could share my bed, but she turned me down.

"Your neighbors will talk no matter what we do."

"Of course, but I don't want them confirming it by seeing two shadows in an upstairs bedroom window." We kissed and I went upstairs, carrying my wadded-up clothes in one hand.

The next morning, I realized how much I missed a comfortable, not quite-fully-dressed conjugal breakfast, helping each other to set places, and serve the meal. In Connecticut, I didn't even have a dog.

"If you're willing to give me the library key, I can finish up with the

Willman collection by myself, Cathy. But if you're not busy, I'd love to have you there with me. We don't even have to talk about Thomas Willman, who, by insider accounts, was a bastard."

Her half smile revealed slightly uneven teeth that I found winsome.

"John, I'm feeling guilty about last night, and hanging out together is maybe not a good idea."

"Please. Don't leave me alone with these mummified books."

Her smile this time was open. "I suppose I have to keep an eye on you so you don't steal any of our valuable volumes."

"Atta girl."

We washed up the breakfast dishes and drove over to the library, where I reviewed the texted appraisals and answered questions that had come in since the day before. There were some other pleasant surprises.

I took flattened cardboard boxes, interleaving sheets and tape out of the SUV, then started folding the boxes into shape and filling them with Willman books. Around noon I drove over to the quick mart, bought a couple drinks and premade sandwiches and brought them back for our lunch. The sandwich bread had the consistency of the cardboard I was assembling.

I started in as we were finishing our colas. "Cathy, I'll be leaving early tomorrow morning, so no breakfast please."

She said nothing, her expression a sad-serious it hurt to see.

"But I hope we can go out to dinner again tonight."

She still said nothing.

"We're so different I think we'd be throwing knives at each other before the end of the month, but I also think you're wonderful."

She stood up in silence and walked over to me, cupping my cheek in her palm. "Have you ever made love in a library?"

"What? No."

"Neither have I. But I've thought about it. There's a skinny sofa in the librarian's office."

I locked the front door and we walked together into the back office. The settee barely had room for two posteriors, let alone two torsos, but we made-do. Afterward, we stuffed the car with book boxes, cleaned up at her house and had another diner dinner. This time I tried with a Greek salad, but I didn't think a Greek would have recognized it.

Once back at Cathy's house we sat on the sofa again, but just talked. For hours. When I finally went up to bed, I'd learned a great deal more about her, but still had to stand outside her viewpoints. She was like a Japanese scroll, with beautifully brushed *kanji* shapes I could admire, without understanding meaning.

In the morning, after coffee, I gave her a gentle goodbye kiss. "I've left a three-volume set on the bed upstairs, Cathy. They're yours to sell. A book a night; seems a fair room rental. There's a card inside the top book from a book appraiser—I've told him you'll be calling."

"You could give the money to the town, but there's not nearly enough to save it. There *is* enough to resuscitate *you*—get a teaching job someplace that deserves you. You could always come back and spend summers here. The winters probably suck anyway."

"You said you were going to keep the books."

"I lied. I needed to see if you knew the books were valuable and were playing me."

Her expression hardened and quickly softened again. "I passed, so *you* made one?"

"Something like that. Whatever you decide, in summer, who knows, maybe I'll call with a yen for your local chicken-fried steak."

She laughed again, and I carried the sound with me out to the car. The smell of old leather and paper permeated the interior on the drive back, reminding me that the rest of the Willman collection would allow indulgence in expensive habits for some time to come.

Edward Ahern is a Vietnam-era U.S. naval officer. He resumed writing after 40-odd years in international sales. He has authored six books, and published more than 250 stories and poems. Ahern is an editor at the on-line journal Bewildering Stories. *Two of his granddaughters are either recent or future graduates of the U.S. Naval Academy.*

Horse-men

By John Thampi
First-Place Poetry (Veteran), 2020

All the hard lessons
my father could have taught me
I learned chasing wild
Horse-men eating daggers in the desert.

If you ask what lesson
I would say the one
your father hid from you
brighten your name
chai tea laced with white milk
make it easy for others to swallow
on breaking down (only at night)
grandfather's prized cane
craven graven images
a horse for a head
steel mixed with clay (as a man should be)
bound your armored wheels
and you screamed *let's go*
learning the intricacies of an ambush
dissolve in the crystalline structure of sucrose
staining the bottom of the vessel
the .50-cal hums
the butterfly trigger rises
when you wake up, raise up your son.

Wake, while it still dark
even as the saucer falls
the ceremonies ignite
a pure thirst
an end to the flare-warmed nights,
echo chambers are your heart
and the wind returns the lesson
the one taught brandishing the sword with the sun

these wild horses are free men
outgunned
we learn to run.

John Thampi was a captain in the U.S. Army Military Police Corps. He deployed twice to Iraq and once to Afghanistan. He left military service in 2012. His writing has appeared in such venues as 9 Lines, The Rialto, Meniscus, Newtown Literary, *Military Experience & the Arts' literary journal* As You Were. *His work has also been anthologized in Oxford Brookes University Poetry Centre's* My Teeth Don't Chew on Shrapnel, *and Southeast Missouri State University's* Proud to Be: Writing by American Warriors, Vol. 5. *In 2019, he was selected to attend the Oxford Brookes Veterans Workshop, and his work was featured in the Oxford Science and Ideas Festival, BBC Radio, and British Forces Broadcasting Service.*

Soldier's Song

By Ben Weakley
Second-Place Poetry (Veteran), 2020

More life exists in the tip
of a bullet smacking
the concrete wall
beside your head

than in a decade spent
commuting to work in traffic,
paying the mortgage on time,
loving a woman and her children,
and taking vacations at the beach.

There is more breath and sweat,
more pulse
and dilating pupil
in the intimate space between
shockwave and steel
debris than you could find
in any lover's fingers.

There is more enlightenment
in the dust cloud
rising from broken asphalt
to drag you underneath
the opened ground
than in a hundred years
of anything else in this life
or the next.

Those who have come close enough
to kiss the painted mask of death–

they have seen millennia.

Ben Weakley spent 14 years in the U.S. Army, including deployments to Iraq and Afghanistan. He lives in the Appalachian Highlands of Northeast Tennessee with his wife, children, and a Redtick hound named Camo. His poetry won first place in the 2019 Heroes' Voices National Poetry Contest. His work appears or is forthcoming in such literary venues as The Ekphrastic Review, Modern Haiku, Vita Brevis, *and* The Wrath-Bearing Tree.

Havoc 58

By Laura Joyce-Hubbard
Third-Place Poetry (Veteran), 2020

small brown paper bags

A burn site on Sheep Mountain,
500 feet from the peak.

*small brown paper bags filled
with*

Nine souls on board. "Jackson,
this is Delta 511. You guys seeing that?"

*small brown paper bags filled
with sleeping pills, tranquilizers,*

A lone, brass trumpet echoes
from back pews in the base chapel.

Wearing my flight suit,
I'm trained to remain dry-eyed.

*small brown paper bags filled
with sleeping pills, tranquilizers, sedatives*

My back throat burning.
We hear them before we see them.

Low overhead. Missing-man
formation honors the dead.

West Texas sky so bright it hurts.

small brown paper bags filled

with sleeping pills, tranquilizers, sedatives

the flight doc passes out

Squinting from the parade ground
to see the space left empty.

Kim was the co-pilot.

Wings on the lead aircraft dip
customary salute to the dead.

small brown paper bags filled
with sleeping pills, tranquilizers, sedatives

the flight doc passes out
to surviving families

Pilot's wife, stumbling in grief,
leans on someone nearby to stand.

Dressed black-drunk.

How, I wonder, did she make
her hair look so beautiful

the morning of her husband's

small brown paper bags filled
with sleeping pills, tranquilizers, sedatives

the flight doc passes out
to surviving families, calls it the prescription

Paper bags damp from palms clenching them.

Laura Joyce-Hubbard graduated from the U. S. Air Force Academy, and piloted C-130s on active duty. She is currently a Master of Fine Arts candidate at Northwestern University. Her awards include a 2020 National Endowment for the Arts (NEA) fellowship to attend the Virginia Center for the Creative Arts (VCCA), nominations for the "2020 AWP Intro Journals Award" in non-fiction and poetry, and finalist recognition for The Iowa Review Award in non-fiction. This poem is dedicated to the aircrew of Havoc 58, which crashed in the vicinity of Jackson Hole, Wyoming Aug. 17, 1996.

Enduring Freedom

By Desiree Cooper
First-Place Prose (Family), 2020

When she turned 12, my big sister Karen decided that I was a pain in the ass. As the baby of the family, I was bewildered at being busted down from Cute Baby Brother to Worthless Gonad by age 6. At school, she deserted me on the playground and pushed me against the lockers if I tried to hug her in the hallway.

The day she flopped in a heap because she had to babysit me, our dad, Chief Master Sgt. Michael Wright, threatened to call the Base Commander to put her in the stockade if she didn't follow orders. That was Dad's joke. He always called mom the "Base Commander."

Karen pouted and complied. But as punishment, she started calling me Weenis (a conflation of "wee" and "penis"), which, every time she said it, cast me into a pit of humiliation. Over time, it was shortened to Ween, which everybody has called me since–even when they toasted me on my wedding day.

I now realize that Karen wasn't being any crueler than most other pre-adolescents are to their younger, pesky, groveling siblings. In fact, maybe I *was* a tad weenish, with my pasty skin and splatter of freckles. The point is that when our family moved to Spangdahlem Air Base in Germany in 2006, I was a fourth-grade misfit, reviled by my own big sister, yearning for a place to belong.

That's when I met Peter Jefferson. He was a stringy fifth-grader–a black kid with coltish limbs and giant feet. While the rest of us wore our bodies awkwardly, Peter sported his lankiness like a promise; it was easy to imagine him growing gloriously into himself by high school. He wore his black hair in a curly nest, untamed, like even his parents couldn't boss him around. His skin was the color of an oiled catcher's mitt, and his grin was both easy and puckish.

Peter was an only child, which may be why he played so easily with kids of any age. After school, he rode bikes with us, or played Enduring Freedom in the field across from the NCO housing. That's how I met him, when I joined his squadron. He asked my name, handed me a plastic grenade, and said, "Sgt. Ween, you take half the men past the ridge," then punched me in the shoulder. I felt like I'd been deputized.

When school was out for the summer, most of us wandered the base on our bikes or skated or lay in the grass, bored. But on some afternoons around four, Peter would grab his kickball and stride to the field. As soon as we spied him standing on the makeshift mound with a white ball wedged beneath his armpit, we came running–just like he was the Pied Piper.

As soon as enough kids gathered on the field, Peter divided us into two teams: the Sabers (after his dad's squadron) and the Warthogs (after the A-10 fighter planes based at Spangdahlem). He mixed the little kids with the bigger ones, the athletic with the awkward. Sometimes one of the boys shed furious tears because his team had too many girls, but Peter would smack the back of his head and say, "Shut up, *scheisskerl*," and the shithead would suck it up and play.

Peter was the boss not only because he was officially in double digits, but also because his dad out-ranked ours. Chief Master Sgt. Jefferson, had deployed twice during Operation Iraqi Freedom. He was an explosive ordinance disposal specialist, which was how Peter knew all about IEDs. Like they could be detonated with garage door openers. Like drones and radio jammers were only 50 percent effective in detecting the enemy planting IEDs or stopping them from exploding. Like dogs were still the best way to sniff one out.

Because the kickball was his and his dad pulled rank, Peter pitched for both teams. Chewing on a wad of watermelon bubblegum, he was a one-man infield, showing off with a lot of lunging and nose-diving into the grass. If anyone missed a kick to the outfield or a base throw, we all yelled "You nutsack!" even at the girls. Peter treated everybody the same.

We usually got through about four innings before the siren blared at five sharp. That's when we all had to stop whatever we were doing– even Peter in mid-pitch–to observe the daily retreat. We'd stand attention with our hands flat against our hearts while they blared the national anthem across the entire air base. If you didn't hide indoors before the siren, you had to stand perfectly still during retreat–even the cars on the road had to stop. If you were caught walking during retreat, the MPs would pull up and give you a warning, or even put you in the back of the squad car.

As soon as all of the flags were retired from their flagpoles and the "Star Spangled Banner" was over, the lucky kickball team would start to cheer. That's because, according to Peter's rules, the team that was up when retreat sounded got an automatic five points. Just like that, losers could become winners–or bigger losers. "Tough tits," Peter said. He was always on the winning team.

One sticky August afternoon when the Sabers were up by five games over the Warthogs, Peter kicked me off his team. "Ween! From now on, you play centerfield for the Hogs," he said, sending me off with a slap on my shoulder. Any other kid would be snot-faced about going to play with the losers, but I was so happy that he'd chosen me to even up the odds. I saluted and took my spot in the field. By the end of the season, every kid had a little whiff of victory.

The Hogs ended the summer two games behind, which felt like a win to us. I started fifth grade that fall not even caring that Karen was now in high school. At school, I gloated whenever Peter, now a sixth-grader, hollered at me while changing classes, "'Sup, Ween?"

Mom complained that I had grown an inch over the summer and needed all new clothes. But it felt like I'd grown more on the inside than the outside. It didn't even faze me when Peter went out for intermural soccer and forgot about us. Well, it would bother me a little when I'd glimpse him running with a pack of sixth-graders in blue and white uniforms, swilling Cokes and teasing girls. But watching him didn't make me feel abandoned, it felt more like I was looking into the future.

"When I'm a sixth-grader," I thought, "I'm going to be like Peter."

Right before Easter, we got the news. Three men from the civil engineer squadron had been killed when an IED exploded beneath a Humvee in Kandahar. Chief Master Sgt. Jefferson had been one of the men in the vehicle. The whole base was shaken. Flags dropped to half-mast.

I cried because Peter's dad was among the dead, but also because I kept imagining that it was my dad. It felt like fate had moved next door. Mom kept giving Dad strange glances, and finally he took me into his arms and promised me that he would always be coming home from his deployments. He made me suck it up and be brave, because Peter's dad had died a hero. I tried, especially when I thought about facing Peter. I didn't want to be wuss when I saw him.

But he never came back to school. I worried that I wouldn't get to say good-bye before his family shipped stateside for the funeral.

About a week after we got the news, I was walking toward the field after school when I noticed a figure already waiting on the mound. The shoulders were a little slumped, but it was definitely Peter. I wanted to break into a run and give him a bear hug. But I stopped as I got close. All of his wild, curly hair was gone. He now had a military buzz.

"Hey?" I said, half in greeting, half in question.

"Hey, Ween," he said, punching me in the stomach. Same old Peter.

We had just counted out teams when three older boys walked up. They were 13-year-olds just transferred from the states, already in their own pack. They were laughing at something I didn't hear, but they stopped dead like gunslingers when they saw us.

"Why you playing with babies, Jefferson?" the tallest one edged up to Peter.

"Yeah," another one chimed in, his face already pocked with acne. Then in a high-pitched voice, he said mockingly, "We want to play!"

We waited for Peter to say something. He hesitated forever, but then shrugged and said, "Sure, you can play." Pointing to the tall one and Mr. Pimples, he said, "You guys are Hogs–first up." Then he pointed to the meatiest one of the three and said, "You're with us. You got first base."

That was my favorite position, but I didn't argue.

"No way," said the tall one, snatching the kickball from Peter. "We aren't playing with you pussies." He and his friends laughed at us, and started to walk away with the ball.

But Peter yelled, "Hey, *scheisskerl,* that's my ball! Give it back."

The kid stopped and faced Peter. "What did you just call me, nigger?"

I stood frozen. Just like that, Peter's face went from anger to the darkest, deepest loss. His friendly smile vanished, his eyes blacked, and his chest caved, like all the wind had been sucked from his lungs. Like he was dead standing up. That look has haunted me so many times since– that moment when you see everything that someone believes in crumble, but you do nothing. The three boys hooted and the tallest threw the ball at Peter. He didn't even try to catch it; he just let it bounce off of his arm and roll to the ground.

Just then, the siren went off. My heart pounded as the national anthem blared, and the whole base went still in respect of our country, our soldiers, our dead. It was a chance to freeze the moment, to figure out what to do. But I never got that chance. As we held still for the retreat, Peter started walking. Everyone watched in shock as, across the whole base, Peter was the only person moving. As he walked away, I wanted to run after him, but I didn't move. None of us did. Instead, I kept my eyes directed toward the sound of the anthem, my hand over my heart.

Desiree Cooper was born in Itazuke, Japan, and spent her entire childhood as a U.S. Air Force dependent. A 2015 Kresge Artist Fellow, Cooper is a Pulitzer Prize-nominated journalist. Her flash-fiction collection, Know the Mother, *has won numerous recognitions, including a 2017 Next Generation Indie Book Award. Her fiction, poetry, and essays have appeared in* The Best Small Fictions 2018, Callaloo, Michigan Quarterly Review, River Teeth, Hypertext Review, Best African American Fiction 2010, *and were noted in* The Best American Essays 2019. *She is currently a full-time caregiver in Virginia for her father, who retired from military service in 1974.*

Countdown to Deployment

By Amy Zaranek

Second-Place Prose (Family), 2020

Ten more days until he is supposed to check out of his command. His waiver goes through–the military has deemed him mission essential. Despite the stop-movement, he can now travel more than 50 miles from home. He can move as if COVID-19 doesn't exist. You tell yourself to take it one day at a time. They're sending your man to the Middle East in the midst of a pandemic.

Nine more days together before he goes. Be happy, tread lightly; he needs you to be strong for him. His family calls a game night when it was supposed to be date night. You remind yourself that he'll be away from them for the next year, too. You look for reassurance at the diamond on your hand in his. He is going unaccompanied for the money, for the time, for being away for one year instead of two accompanied. If he loves it, and if you love it when you visit, maybe you'll elope in a chapel on base.

He rolls over you on the morning of Day Eight. The breeze through the window and the rain on the street makes you forget he has to go. You laugh together and nuzzle noses and whisper your love. In the afternoon, he receives guidelines from his next duty station: a greeting in Arabic from U.S. Naval Forces Central Command. He reads it with a smile; you read disbelief and excitement in his crinkling eyes. He will be tested for COVID when he arrives in Bahrain, then will be quarantined on base or in a marble-floored four-star hotel eating food from the galley or 24-hour room service. He will be tested again after two weeks. He looks forward to the adventure of foreign quarantine. You worry that the pandemic will prevent you from seeing him while he's gone. You make your life more mobile.

The night before Day Seven is sad. At 1 a.m., you cry, burying your face in his chest. You don't want him to go. He holds you and kisses your forehead and rubs your back, and you worry that you're adding to his stress. He's done this for 18 years, but you never have. You wake with swollen eyes and a headache. He wakes and goes to his work computer. His orders come through, but they're wrong–sending him to a training still closed for months due to coronavirus. He makes calls and checks his e-mail. In the afternoon, the two of you go to the convenience store to buy more masks.

On Day Six, you watch Netflix together and wait for his order modification. There are less than 48 hours until he's supposed to check out at headquarters. You sit close, keeping both hands on him, as if to soak up all the times you won't be able to touch him. You feel lucky to be quarantined with him here, that he wasn't already deployed when all this started. At night, he reads jokes to you from his phone. You record his laughter. The video picks up nothing but soft sound and darkness; you know you'll replay it again and again and again when he's gone.

Day Five: he receives his order modification while FaceTiming with the officer he'll replace overseas. You eat breakfast at the kitchen table, trying not to eavesdrop or jump to conclusions. You go to the other room where it's harder to hear him. You know he'll fill you in truthfully. He's told you how OPTEMPO picks up closer to sea duty, especially one this arduous. You start to understand when you see him switching between work phone and personal, texts and calls, updating you in between. You pack your bags in minutes and get ready to drive three hundred miles to headquarters with him. He knocks on the door when you're in the shower and tells you his orders have changed again. Now he's going to Norfolk before Bahrain. Two ORDMODs in a morning. His detailer says it isn't even a record in this unprecedented time. You stay strong, you stay flexible, you support him. You feel like you've aged a decade in the past three months and another five years today.

You wake early on Day Four to the sound of the air conditioner and his light snoring as the big spoon. You are frustrated–your plans have changed six times in the past twenty-four hours, and you long for some semblance of normalcy. Maybe this morning will be the most normal for the next year. There was a shooting on the base in Corpus Christi, and you tell him to stay safe in Norfolk. You tell him how you want everything to be perfect before he goes, so you raise the bar and beat yourself up over your smallest mistakes. You tell him you don't want to be a statistic, not another failed military relationship. He lifts your spirits with a pep talk: it's not what happens that determines success, it's your reaction. The fact that you're communicating about frustration is already a sign of success. The two of you have moved out of your apartment and with nowhere else to stay, you check into a hotel. You make love. The ceiling leaks. When you switch rooms, you snuggle and laugh and snack until 3 a.m.

Your mind races on the morning of day three, which may now be Day Two or Four or Day 18 and you aren't sure why you're keeping track anymore. You try to make plans for the days before he leaves. None of it is in your control. You want him to go so he can hurry up and get back; so you can marry him. You want him to stay so you won't miss a moment with him. When asked what you'll do when he's gone, you come up with hypotheticals, but nothing in stone. You just finished your MFA and might edit, might teach, might fill in on the farm where you used to work, but none of it seems consuming enough to keep your mind off of his absence. So you focus on his presence. You focus on the moment. The rest will come in time. Besides, you want to be free enough to be with him whenever and wherever you can. You hope COVID will permit. You've talked about Paris and Dubai; he's talked about coming home for Christmas. You talk about restaurants you'll go together when he comes back and your state reopens. Now, you share each meal and split each dish. When he passes the hotel fork to you, you shovel too-large bites into your small mouth. He eats quickly, having learned in the galley and on the carrier. You've learned to keep up.

On Day Two, you long for alone-time. You wish you could stick to something you say you'll do. There are no more slow mornings or quiet days. He senses your gloom and sits in the car with you and asks if you want to talk. You need a minute, but follow him into his parents' house to celebrate his birthday two months late. The company cheers you in a departure from your introversion. The two of you drive to his brother's house singing along with old Taylor Swift and classic rock. He and his brother play a board game of their own invention while you sit in the other room, working on writing and stealing glances at your man, savoring each look and wishing you could bottle them for all the times he's more than one room away. You hug him in the kitchen while making a midnight snack. The nights keep getting later but this is your second day in a row without crying.

It's Day One. Sunday of Memorial Day weekend. You've never been sure if the holiday honors all veterans or focuses on the fallen. Mere weeks ago, you followed COVID protocols like a religion. Now, the pandemic is the furthest thing from your mind as you hug your goodbyes and hold hands in prayer. In the parking lot of his storage unit, you share McNuggets and listen to "Chicken Fried" and don't realize the coincidence until later, opting to stay in the moment. You help him clean out his car and push a cart of storage totes down the dimly lit hall. When he rolls up the door to his locker, you see your life together deconstructed: your mattress leaning against the wall, your couch shoved into the corner, your kitchen chairs piled on top of your coffee table. You know you could feel sad about locking your furniture away. Instead, you look forward to moving all of it into your next home together. At the end of the day, you thank him for all he does. This could be the last night you share for a while. *It's nice to be appreciated,* he says.

Day Zero—what was supposed to be Day Zero. You're in limbo. It's uncertain when his orders will come through and when he can check out and when he can fly. He decides it's time to go to headquarters to be ready to go at a moment's notice. You pack his and your bags into your truck. His car was left behind for family use in his absence. The two of you make one last trip to the storage unit. He drops off his old flight helmet and recruiting awards. You say one last goodbye to his parents, you pick up breakfast sandwiches at your favorite local coffee shop, and you drive to Detroit past freshly sprouted farm fields. He DJs on your phone and naps in the passenger seat. You wish you could bottle the sunshine on your arms, his soft breathing asleep and laughter awake, the air conditioning on your bare toes, the togetherness. In the evening, you squeeze in an engagement photo session outside of the ballpark where he proposed. You share Easy Mac for dinner on your parents' couch in the suburbs. That night, you lay fully clothed above the sheets in accordance with their conservatism. It is too hot, the windows are open, you're wrapped around his left side, and despite your restlessness, you wouldn't change anything. You barely sleep. You whisper late into the night about future plans to visit, telling him you love him whenever the conversation stops. As a couple, you always make the best of things. When you drift off, you dream of storms.

Day Zero again. He rolls out of bed early to check his e-mail and his orders haven't come through at start of business. The time difference between headquarters and detailer accounts for it. You fold his laundry and make his coffee–tasks he usually does for himself, but you want to take any weight off his back that you can. You wish you could carry it all for him. An hour later, his orders arrive. His expected departure date is listed as yesterday. He rolls his luggage into the driveway and says goodbye to your mom, and you all take photos. You drive him to headquarters. He holds your hand. He reassures you sweetly and tears rise behind your sunglasses. *No fair getting misty eyes while you're driving,* he says, and hands you a tissue. *I'll save all the mushy stuff for later.* You assume later means at the airport that evening. At headquarters, he starts the command checkout process while his boss gives you a tour of the office. The wardroom greets you with congratulations and genuineness built over the last two years. You sit across from flags and trophies in the lobby and you write about the day. You can hear his voice drifting from each office he visits. His words are unintelligible but you savor the sound. Right now, he is still close enough that you could rest your head against his chest and feel him speak: you've done it so many times that you know exactly how the deepness of his voice rumbles in his chest. He receives his end-of-tour award and shakes hands with the skipper despite social distancing. You drive him back to your parents' house and wait for his itinerary. You play games with your family. Friends stop by to see him off. They keep their distance in the driveway and wish him well for when he goes. His itinerary never arrives; he cannot leave.

Every day is Day Zero now. All the steps are completed except the final one that will send him away. He could get an e-mail at any time that would cut your seemingly-endless stretch of togetherness into a few hours: a drive to the airport, a teary farewell. You bask in the unknown time you have left. The evenings feel the freest. The offices are closed so you won't receive any news for the next 16 hours. You take him to your favorite hometown sandwich shop and show him your dream home down the street. You feel deeply present in the evening's golden light. You build a bonfire in the backyard. It burns fast and hot and you sit and talk until the glowing embers fade to black.

On the next Day Zero, he bets you that he'll hear something today. You agree, but you've felt that way for days. You've stopped wondering when the "last" will be–the last day, the last night, the last meal–you don't know. It's a constant course of uncertain goodbyes. He calls it a "spin cycle" and you call it a "roller coaster." He tells you that you seem to be handling everything better this week than last. You agree. He keeps mentioning how much he wants to get started on everything there. Movement will ease his worry. You want him to go so he can get started on coming back. By the end of the day, there is still no news.

The suspension of time swirls back to reality with a phone call three days after checkout. He is to leave the next morning. He goes with you to ask your cousin to be the maid of honor in your post-deployment wedding. She says *of course* just like you did three months earlier, when he asked you to marry him. He arranges his flights and, on the way home, runs down a timeline for the evening. He makes steak for dinner, one of your favorite traditions as a couple. You eat on the balcony in the treetops and walk your dog together in the evening. You never thought you could feel this sort of happiness in your hometown and you know that you'll feel it again and even greater in the next place you call home with him. Dark thoughts nag as dusk settles and you tell him *I know you're not going to leave, but all of my relationships have ended in situations like this.* Your dog sniffs at the grass. He squeezes your hand and tells you that he's not going to do anything to mess this up; he put a ring on your finger and he's coming back to you. You wrap your arms around his shoulders at the corner and the scene behind him–your family's home, the fading light–blurs through tears that you don't let fall. He wipes at your dry eyes. You're trying to save your sadness for morning.

It's your last night together for a while, and you want it to be happy. For the last few weeks–hell, his second half of shore duty–all the serious talks and tears led up to this night. It is somber but not emotional. It is unspoken. It is enough. You drape your arm over his waist and press your body to his back. You count down the hours and hold him close.

You drive west across the city before dawn, his bags packed into the back of your truck. The two of you roll his luggage from short-term parking to the terminal. You joke that he looks like a Batman villain with his shaved head and mask. The check-in line looks long because of social-distancing; it moves quickly. He puts his bags on the scale. The woman at the counter asks you if you're traveling today. *Not yet,* you say. You look down. *But really soon,* he adds. You touch his arm. Before security, he takes off his mask. He pulls your face to his and kisses you. Unlike the sweet smooches you've shared all morning, this one is serious. Urgent. This one is saying goodbye. You rest your foreheads against each other. His sunglasses press into your chest and mascara stains your sweatshirt sleeve. He rubs your back and holds you close to him. *I'd better get going,* he says. *I'll see you so soon. It's you and me. I love you.* You watch him walk to security; somewhere you can't follow. He zigzags through the empty maze to the back of the line. You stand still.

He sets down his heavy bag and you don't know how long to stand and watch. It could be all day, or it could already be too long. You blow him a kiss and turn away. You wave from the escalator and look at him until the ceiling hides him from view. When you imagined this scene weeks ago, it was a wiped tear and your ring glinting in the sun– something pretty, almost romantic, a reminder of hope. In reality, you cry all the way back to the parking structure and sit in your truck for an extra half-hour. The radio turns on automatically to a too-happy country song. You turn it down. Someday, these songs will sound jubilant again. You blow your nose into a rough paper towel and your eyes are already swollen in the rearview. Your chest is tight and your throat is raw from gasping for air. You wonder how you'll drive home. The parking structure is empty and you follow the exit signs like a detour. You drive into a neon orange sun rising above the city where you were born and find beauty in this departure. Now, the days will count upward until you know when he's coming home again. Day One.

Amy Zaranek holds a Master of Fine Arts degree in creative non-fiction from Ashland University. She is the managing editor of the Black Fork Review. *Her writing focuses on issues of sustainability, agriculture, and military relationships, and has appeared in such venues as* Yemassee Journal, matchbook, *and* honey & lime. *In her personal life, Zaranek is engaged to be married to U.S. Navy Lt. Jason Gaidis. For more information about her work, visit: www.amyzaranek.com.*

The Favorite Hour

By Meredith Wadley

Third-Place Prose (Family), 2020

I. A Pleasant Evening

Cool, post-rain gusts blew off the Lake of Zurich. Olivia, heading home from work, paused at an art gallery window. The glass reflected the tree-lined street's confetti of leaflitter, their greens, gray-greens, ochres, and rusts plastered to the sidewalk–but the colors weren't reflections, after all. The colors came from behind the glass, where 12 unframed paintings, dreamlike landscapes brushed onto the rough sides of pressboards, hung three down and four across.

She lingered. If she missed the next tram, no worries. No one waited for her at home, the husband an ex, the son grown. When, actually, was the last time she'd had Pascal, her son, over?

She held up her phone to photograph the paintings, thinking they might inspire something. But phone screens altered images. Where a moment ago, she saw through the reflections to see paintings, now she saw reflections of the languid current of pedestrians, a cyclist spiriting past, and the street's London plane trees sparkling in a rogue shaft of sunlight.

Leaves shimmered. Drops of water pattered the sidewalk behind her. She lowered her phone and stepped inside. The gallerist, a young woman, sat behind a large wooden table in the corner farthest from the door, her face half-hidden by a tearful sweep of pink orchid blossoms.

"*Grüzi,*" Olivia said in greeting. An American graphic designer nearly 30 years living in Zurich, she spoke its dialect, *Züriitüütsch*, and dressed Swiss-like; today, mustard suede mules–impractical for the rain–black three-quarter cashmere slacks, and a knitted duster over a pressed white shirt. Staying in dialect, she asked to photograph the paintings.

"*Bitte schön,*" the gallerist said. The room's parsimony amplified her soft voice, and she added that this hour was her favorite in the gallery; the evening light. She moved to the front of the table and half-sat upon it. Dressed in an elegant navy A-line dress, powder-blue felt bobbles, and a severe chignon, she looked ready to join a cocktail party. "The artist worked from film footage he found on YouTube. Home movies American soldiers in Vietnam had filmed in the Sixties."

Taken aback, Olivia lowered her phone. Vietnam, here. What place could be more removed from her childhood experiences of Vietnam than a gallery in Zurich, Switzerland? She narrowed her eyes, trying to make sense of the paintings' blurred landscapes, and unwittingly mumbled in English, "The war."

"Oh, you are American?" the gallerist asked, switching into English.

Olivia nodded.

She'd grown up military, and when she was 8, her daddy had spent a year in Vietnam. Not that she remembered much about the absence, really. There'd been so many antecedents to it–days, weeks, months when he'd been gone. That year had been marked by postcards and packages arriving from Saigon and her grandparents coming to babysit so her parents could spend a week together in Hawaii. As she recalled it, where they'd lived at the time, in Fayetteville, North Carolina, his absence wasn't the only absence that was, had been, or would be. Plenty of fathers in the neighborhood had gone to work in uniform.

The gallerist now stood next to her. "Julian–the artist–would stop frames to paint, which is why they are all out of focus. It's a lovely effect." They reminded Olivia of news footage she'd seen on their TV nightly, sandbags and explosions, green jungles and muddy rivers. Shoulder-high grasses and wounded soldiers being loaded onto helicopters.

"Here," the gallerist said, "um–what's it called, *eine Sprengung*?"

"A detonation."

"Yes?"

Olivia resisted the urge to touch the painting, its showers of reddish browns.

On the tram, trundling homewards, a memory emerged, of watching coverage of an attack on an airfield, dirt and debris showering a C-123. Her mother had covered her mouth as the plane had begun–sloth-like– to back from the edge of the blast hole.

The tram slowed, and she understood now the gasp her mother had made: Daddy had piloted a C-123–General Westmoreland's–and they might have been watching him under fire.

II. Unwrapped

Olivia mounted a walnut picture-rail. On it, she set her trio of paintings and began trawling YouTube to locate each frame depicted, the hurling wind of a Huey's liftoff, an explosive dispersion of sand and gravel, and a red-clay airstrip with sentinel landing signals, round and faceless.

Filled with a predator's tingle of game and play, she wondered if these very places might have been familiar to Daddy. Success baited her pleasure as she found one image after the other. Being alone dampened her mood somewhat. She thought of Pascal, but never mind her son being with her. She wouldn't have known how to explain the quiescent emotions the paintings awakened or the thrill of pinpointing each image's source. She'd rarely spoken of the war or her military upbringing to him, after all—what was Vietnam to a Swiss kid?

Four months before Olivia's departure for Switzerland, newly married and carrying Pascal, cancer had taken her daddy. He'd never spoken about his experiences and never asked about hers.

Closing the tab on YouTube, she thought of Lisa, her best friend from those Fayetteville days. Their daddies being in Vietnam at the same time, the girls had bonded; never mind that Olivia's daddy had well out-ranked Lisa's, the two had sat together on the school bus, played together at each other's houses, and had sleepovers, not paying attention to the war coverage on each other's TV, giggling and joking until shushed by one or the other of their anxious mothers.

The friendship had not survived the death of Lisa's daddy. The military kids on their street and school bus had bullied Lisa—as if her loss were a personal weakness or a character flaw or a contagion—and Olivia, lacking the skills and courage to interfere, had withdrawn. Somehow, the experience had cost Olivia her carefree self.

What was it, old friends had remarked about her having a "bombproof remoteness?" What Pascal's father had called an "impenetrable indifference?" Well, she supposed there were things in her life she avoided examining. Unraveling. Recovering from. Perhaps her ex should see her now, in possession of something to share, anxious, and flushed. She touched the brush of ochre on one of the boards as if touching her Daddy's cheek and decided to reach out to her son. To a photograph of the picture rail and paintings, she added a voice message,

"Stop by this weekend? These have a story I want to share with you. And I miss you."

III. The Bridge

Olivia and Pascal sat at her dining table. At its center, an Advent wreath, four candles burning, gave off a pine scent, and the fresh tea in their mugs added undertones of apples and spices.

Through the living room's balcony doors, the December afternoon's soft light seeped, her view of the lake and Alps a foggy distance. She'd shared much about Daddy, Pascal patiently listening and asking questions, and perhaps it was too much, sharing the events following his kidney failure–many years after his retirement from service–but she couldn't help herself, and Pascal hadn't stopped her.

"The chemo had knocked out a kidney. The oncologists hoped the big hospital could save the surviving kidney; surgery wasn't an option." An ambulance was due to transfer him, and Oliva was there to take along his personal effects.

"He suffered delusions. Transfixed by a cheesy print of a weeping willow and an arched wooden bridge that hung on the wall, he babbled nonsense about the 'Wheel of Life.'"

Curled, fetal-like, in his bed, he quivered, his forehead hot, his skin as soft and dry as a moth's wing. When Olivia tried covering him with a sheet or blanket, he'd bark about the pain of being touched.

"How old was he?" Pascal asked.

"Sixty. But he looked 90, his leathery face as creased and bristled as Peat Bog Man. I was half his age and had just met your dad."

Pascal's dad had excited her like a new destination could, and she thought he'd be the one she wouldn't tire of–she'd gone through relationships like the family had gone through transfers, averaging 18 months before moving on. Ironic, then, that her ex had been the one to drift, drawn to living deep within the Alps; Olivia preferred seeing the mountains from a distance. "He'd also say, 'We have no business being there,' meaning Vietnam. God knows what he was wrestling with."

Pascal stood. "I'm listening," he said, picking up an ashtray and a packet of cigarettes. He opened the balcony door and stepped outside. Cold air swept around the loft. The ornaments on Olivia's Christmas tree tinkled, and the flames on her advent wreath blew out.

Between her phone message to Pascal about the paintings and this post-Christmas visit, several weeks had passed. He'd spent the holiday with his dad and Swiss relations. And he'd offered to spend Silvester with her, but he was better off with friends, so she'd turned him down.

"Go on," he said.

"Two paramedics arrived," she said, her voice raised. "They tried disconnecting Daddy's drip and removing his clamps, but he yelled at them to leave him alone." Disease had reduced him to a child, allowing him no dignity. "I'd never seen him so vulnerable."

Except she had, during the first church services with Daddy after his return from Vietnam. He'd wept in silence. When Olivia nudged her mom, she was cautioned to "leave him alone." Now, the recollection of that moment on the pew and her confusion silenced her.

Pascal stepped back inside. A slipstream of fog followed him, dissolving immediately. He poured fresh tea and relit the candles.

"Daddy started shouting, 'They're killing our children!' and one of the paramedics raised his hands as if being mugged. I tried calming him down; I knew exactly what he meant."

She asked if Pascal knew about the Kent State shootings. "When the National Guard opened-fire on students protesting the invasion of Cambodia?"

"Yes."

"We were living in Ohio then, a few hours' drive south of the campus. We'd moved there just after Daddy got back from Vietnam. He was so angry about the war–would say we had no business being over there–and the students' anti-war rallies really got his attention."

"He sided with them?"

"Said the real purpose of our involvement was so top brass could climb the ranks."

She gripped her teacup. "We were watching the protest coverage together, Daddy perched on his recliner. Tense. The news footage captured students and guardsmen milling about–and then teargas, *crack, crack, crack*, and screaming, scattering students. Daddy jumped to his feet. Shouted, 'Now they're killing our children!'"

"How old were you?" Pascal asked.

"Almost 10."

"Did he frighten you?"

"Yes. I think he did. But I wasn't feeling fear in the hospital–I was just anxious for those poor paramedics. Every time they tried lifting the corners of Daddy's bedsheet to shift him, he'd yell and swat at them—despite the effort being clearly very painful. Finally I said, 'Daddy, these men are following orders. It's their duty to get you onto the gurney.'"

"One said, 'Yes, sir,' and saluted.

"That got Daddy's attention. He looked at the men and then at me, the whites of his eyes piss yellow. God, he was sick, yet in that moment, lucid. 'Men,' he said with an officer's nod. And that was that."

"He survived the kidney failure."

"But not the cancer. Six months later, he was dead."

Pascal glanced at the paintings. "I like them, their colors, and how the evening light fames them. The one with rounded forms—it's a bridge?"

"An airstrip."

"I appreciate knowing the context."

"Someday they'll be yours, I guess."

"Not soon, I hope." Pascal smiled.

"I'm the age Daddy was when he died."

Her son reached for her hands and held them.

"You have his smile, you know," Olivia said.

In the darkening room, her son's eyes reflected the flickers of the Advent candle flames. She glanced at the paintings. They had found her. Found her for a reason.

Meredith Wadley is a former U.S. Air Force brat, who lives and works in a medieval microtown on the Swiss side of the Rhine River. She is at work on a collection of stories about military-family life in the Vietnam War era. Her fiction is published or forthcoming in such venues as Bandit Fiction, Collateral, Disquiet Arts, Gone Lawn, JMWW, Lammergeier, Longleaf Review, Lunate Fiction, Orca Lit, *and* upstreet. *For more information, visit: www.meredithwadley.com.*

Pursuit

By Lisa Stice
First-Place Poetry (Family), 2020

for Martha Gellhorn

Is anything ever an accident?
Being at the wrong place at the wrong
time on a barstool in Key West, air thick,
and words smooth as whiskey neat.

Sometimes home is not a home, sometimes
love is on a beach in Normandy
where you're not supposed to be, but love
is a journal and a pencil, the scratch of witness.

Who is anyone to tell you what to do?
From Havana to the Italian Front, from
Finland, Burma, England, Singapore,
after your ocean voyage, that was enough of him.

Sometimes home is not a home, sometimes
love was never really there reading
the evening paper or typing at a desk, but
think of this: he's your footnote now.

Author's note: Martha Gellhorn (1908-1998) was a U.S. novelist
(whose works included *Stricken Field, The Wine Astonishment / Point of
No Return, and His Own Man*); war correspondent (for publications
that included *Collier's Weekly, The Atlantic Monthly, The Face of War,
The Lowest Trees Have Tops,* and *Vietnam: A New Kind of War*); and
travel writer (*Travels with Myself* and *Another*). She was also the third
wife of Ernest Hemingway.

Lisa Stice is a poet, mother, and military spouse. She is the author of two full-length collections, Permanent Change of Station *(2018) and* Uniform *(2016), and a chapbook,* Desert *(2018). While it is difficult to say where home is, she currently lives in North Carolina with her husband, daughter and dog. For more information about her writing, visit: lisastice.wordpress.com.*

Dancing with my Father

By Ellyana Gomez
Second-Place Poetry (Family), 2020

Dance with me
Because a very long day has passed
And the only thing
Between your return here
And the last return
Was the hands of God

For many months
I smiled at the moon,
To the kind face that we share each night
And I sent you my kisses through her
I have prayed for you ceaselessly
Every free minute I had was dedicated to your safety

Dance with me
Because I missed you so much
And I have shared my hero
For too many months
With the other side of the world
Now I want to be selfish
I want more time with you
Because I almost lost it forever
But you're already mine, you're ours again

I missed you so much
With all my little heart
Everything you've seen doesn't matter to me
Everything you have done does not affect my idea of you
Your soul has guided me
For all of my life
Now you guide again with your steps and your wisdom

Dance with me please

Because I want to celebrate your return
And every one of your steps
With every beat of the drums

Ellyana Gomez is currently enrolled in the School of Social Work at the University of Pittsburgh. She has developed her love of poetry since she was a child, exploring Maya Angelou and Langston Hughes poems with her father. She continues to write about her lived experiences, and her observations of current events and art. She has been published in several anthologies and journals, including Poetry Quarterly, *and was recently awarded the "Best in School" award at the Carnegie Mellon Martin Luther King Jr. Day Writing Awards.*

An Offering

By Michael Janairo
Third-Place Poetry (Family), 2020

I.
The dark husks of a halved coconut
held steaming slices of roast pork,
purple rice cakes, green bataw beans,
and a bouquet of white blossoms
from fresh-cut sampaguita, all carried
in the outstretched hands of a boy
leading men and bancas to the sea.

He waded into waist-high water
and pushed the Diwata's offering away
and watched it wobble on the surface
until it disappeared into the deep,
a payment for the ancient sea spirit
to guide and protect the fishermen
as they paddled into their day's work.

The boy, as his ancestors before him,
stayed in the surf and hoped to glimpse
the one who took the foods that left
his mouth watering and who brought
the men home with a bounty of fish,
his small body tight in anticipation
that she would rise, a dazzling light,
like Christ, The White Lady of the Sea.

II.
Fevered, he paddles out to sea
weakened by malarial shakes,
the high-sun tropical heat,
he doesn't rest until his
shore-line home is lost from view

He stifles a cough
Japanese voices carry
shouting at his wife and child
to stay outside as soldiers
search for anything, though he
would be the prize, and the papers
stashed in a valise at his feet.

More voices—wife? child?—
his fevered body shudders
and thinks of dark coconut husks,
sliced pork, rice cakes, bataw beans,
and wishes to teach his boy
about offerings to the sea spirit,
but what need has he, a city child,
trembling, for a diwata at a time of war?

His ill chest heaves with such violence
he cannot contain his coughs,
wracking across the waves, he fears
all will be lost, save for a sudden presence
breaking the sea's solemn surface,
crowned with white blossoms
and rivulets of flowing hair,
cascades of noisy splashes,
like frenzied bangús taking to air,
mask his hacks and when,
his heaving chest relaxed,
he mouths his thanks, but
the White Lady of the Sea is gone,
leaving a bright sun, still blue sky
and ebbing Japanese voices
as the patrol moves on from
his home, wife, child and sea.

Michael Janairo is a former U.S. Army brat whose father, uncle, and lolo *(Filipino for "grandfather") were all West Point graduates and career officers. He earned a Master of Fine Arts degree in writing from the University of Pittsburgh, and an undergraduate degree in journalism at Northwestern University. His poetry and fiction have been published in numerous literary journals, and is forthcoming in* Event *and* Weirdbook *magazines. His Filipino family name is pronounced "ha-NY-row." For more information on his work, visit: michaeljanairo.com.*

Glossary

Writing about the military often involves acronyms and initialisms. Acronyms are abbreviations that are read as words; initialisms are abbreviations that are read as individual letters. Further confusing the issue, some terms can be read as either. With all that as context, we've listed and informally defined below some pronunciations and definitions of jargon found in this book:

A.N.A.: Afghan National Army

A.S.A.P.: "As Soon As Possible." Sometimes pronounced "AY-sap."

A.T.M.: Automated Teller Machine

BATS ("Bats"): Biometric Automated Toolkit System. A portable set of hardware used by soldiers to measure and record phyiscal characteristics of civilians and combatants (examples: iris scans and fingerprints), which can later be used for identification.

B.E.T.: Black Entertainment Television

CATCC ("KAT-see-see"): Carrier Air Traffic Control Center. The entity that manages take-offs and landings aboard a U.S. aircraft carrier, as well as the airspace around the ship.

C.B.: Citizens-Band. A publicly accessible radio frequency band used by truckers and others for communications.

C.O.: Corrections Officer. A prison employee.

COMSEC ("KAHM-sehk"): Communications Security. Measures and controls taken to deny unauthorized persons information derived from telecommunications and to ensure the authenticity of such telecommunications. A "COMSEC key" ensures that only parties with matching codes can receive, transmit, and/or understand a given communication.

COP ("Kop"): Combat Outpost. A small patrol base.

COVID ("KOH-vid"): Coronavirus. A family of respiratory viruses.

DEROS ("Deer-ROHS"): "Date Estimated Return from Overseas." Vietnam War-era acronym regarding the date at which an individual military service member would be eligible to return home from wartime deployment.

D.J.: "Disc Jockey." The act of performatively selecting and playing recorded music, or a person who performs that function.

DD-214 ("Dee-Dee-Two-Fourteen"): A standardized U.S. Department of Defense form issued to miitary service members upon separation from active-duty, which summarizes dates of service, awards, and other achievments. In conversation, often used as shorthand for "proof of veteran status."

D.M.Z.: "Demilitarized Zone." Territory in dispute between fighting forces.

D.U.I.: "Driving Under the Influence." A moving violation. Depending on the state, also "Driving While Intoxicated" (D.W.I.) or "Operating While Intoxicated" (O.W.I.)

E.C.P.: Entry Control Point. The guarded and barricaded entrance to a FOB, COP, or other military installation.

E.M.: "Enlisted Men's"

E.P.W.: Enemy Prisoner of War

FOB ("FAHB"): Forward Operating Base. A larger tactical base from which one or more miltiary units may stage operations. Bigger than a COP.

G.I.: "Government Issue." A slang term for U.S. soldier.

H.Q.: Headquarters

I.D.: Infantry Division

I.E.D.: Improvised Explosive Device. A landmine manufactured from parts not expresssly made for that purpose.

JSOC ("JAY-sock"): Joint Special Operations Command

Klick: Sometimes "click." Military slang for a kilometer (km) of distance.

L.A.: Los Angeles, California

Medevac ("MED-eh-vack"): "Medical Evacuation"

M.F.A. Master of Fine Arts. A type of graduate degree, often in creative writing, poetry, and other literary forms.

MRAP ("EHM-rap"): Mine-Resistant, Ambush-Protected truck. A family of tactical and wheeled armored vehicles.

M.R.E.: "Meal, Ready-to-Eat." A type of single-serving field ration issued by the U.S. military.

M.P.: Military Police

MP5 ("Ehm-pee-five"): A type of German-manufactured submachine gun, widely used by law enforcement and military organizations.

N.V.A.: North Vietnamese Army

N.V.G.: Night-vision Goggles

OPTEMPO ("AHP-tem-poh"): "Operational Tempo." The frequency with which military operations or missions occur.

ORDMOD ("ORD-MAHD"): "Order Modification."

P.F.C.: Private First Class. The second-lowest rank in the U.S. Army. Also abbreviated "Pfc."

P.O.W.: Prisoner of War

PREP ("Prehp"): Prison Rape Elimination Plan

P.R.T.: Provincial Reconstruction Team

Q.R.F.: Quick-Reaction Force

R&R: "Rest and Recuperation." Sometimes also "Rest and Relaxation" or "Rest and Recreation."

R.P.G.: Rocket-Propelled Grenade

SERE ("SEER-ee"): Survival, Evasion, Resistance, and Escape. A training program for military personnel on how to avoid and escape capture.

S.O.P.: Standing Operating Procedure

S.U.V.: Sport Utility Vehicle

TACAN ("TAY-kan"): Tactical Air Navigation. A radio system used by military pilots to determine the range and bearing of their aircraft.

T.C.: "Tank / Track / Truck Commander." The person nominally in charge of a given tactical vehicle.

U.M.R.: "University of Missouri at Rolla"

V.C.: Viet Cong. The insurgent guerilla force that fought U.S. and South Vietnamese forces in the Vietnam War.

V.H.F.: "Very High Frequency." A VHF radio is a Frequency Modulated (FM) radio used for two-way voice communications, named after the band of frequencies in which it operates.

Vic ("Vihk"): Army slang for "vehicle."

X.O.: "Executive Officer." A secondary leader in a military unit, often tasked with managing administration, maintenance, and logistics.

Col. Darron L. Wright
Memorial Writing Awards

Adminstered annually by the Chicago-based literary journal *Line of Advance* since 2016, and underwritten by the philanthropic Blake & Bailey Family Fund, the Col. Darron L. Wright Memorial Writing Awards have recognized excellence in prose (includes fiction, non-fiction, and hybrid forms) and poetry by U.S. military service members and veterans.

In 2020, Wright Award organizers announced additional prose and poetry categories for immediate family members of U.S. military service members and veterans.

The awards commemorate a U.S. Army leader and author who was killed in a September 2013 parachute training accident. Darron L. Wright, 45, had deployed three times to Iraq, and was author of a 2012 memoir *Iraq Full Circle: From Shock and Awe to the Last Combat Patrol in Baghdad and Beyond*.

Cash prizes of $250, $150, and $100 are awarded in each "service member/veteran" and "family" group, for a total of four categories.

The 2020 guest judge was Katey Schultz, author the 2013 short-story collection *Flashes of War* and the 2019 Afghan War novel *Still Come Home*.

For more information, visit:

URL: www.lineofadvance.org/colonel-darren-l-wright-contest

About the Editor

Christopher Lyke is a writer and teacher living in Chicago. He served in Afghanistan and Africa as an enlisted infantry soldier with the U.S. Army. He is the founding editor for the non-profit *Line of Advance*, an on-line literary journal for veterans. He can usually be found running with his dog in Logan Square or watching the Buckeyes at Vaughan's Pub. Lyke has been published in such venues as *BlazeVOX* and Military Experience & the Arts' literary journal *As You Were*. In 2015, he won the short-story award in *Proud to Be: Writing by American Warriors, Vol. 4.*

Line of Advance recognizes the need for fellow veterans to tell their stories, and for the public to read them. The journal is committed to the idea that times of war are transformative for a nation, and that the act of telling stories creates opportunities for introspection, empathy, and mutual understanding.

Since 2016, underwritten by the philanthropic Blake & Bailey Family Fund, the Chicago-based literary publication has administered the Col. Darron L. Wright Memorial Writing Awards.

For more information about *Line of Advance*, visit:

URL: www.lineofadvance.org

Twitter: @lineofadvance

About the Cover Designer

Established by freelance designer Paul Hewitt, Battlefield Design was born out of a life-long fascination with military history. This passion, along with more than 25 years in graphic design, enables us to approach each task with a creative eye and an understanding of the subject to produce effective, eye-catching results.

We work in all areas of graphic design, including logos, branding, brochures, advertising, and display graphics. What sets us apart is our work for military history publishers, film-makers, museums and tour operators all over the world. We produce material including maps, tour guides, books, museum displays and illustrations covering wars and conflicts throughout history.

For more information about Battlefield Design, visit:

URL: www.battlefield-design.co.uk

E-mail: info@battlefield-design.co.uk

Twitter: @BattlefieldGD

Did You Enjoy This Book?

Tell your friends and colleagues about it, or post your thoughts via social media sites, like Facebook and Twitter! On-line communities that serve military families, veterans, and service members are also ideal places to help spread the word about this book, and others like it!

You can also share a quick review on websites for other readers, such as Goodreads.com. Or offer a few of your impressions on bookseller websites, such as Amazon.com and BarnesandNoble.com!

Better yet, recommend the title to your favorite local librarian, book club leader, museum gift store manager, or independent bookseller! There is nothing more powerful in business of publishing than a shared review or recommendation from a friend.

We appreciate your support! We'll continue to look for new stories and voices to share with our readers. Keep in touch!

You can write us at:

Middle West Press LLC
P.O. Box 31099
Johnston, Iowa 50131-9428

Or visit: www.middlewestpress.com

Made in the USA
Middletown, DE
14 October 2020